REXX:
Tools and Techniques

Books from QED

Database

Managing IMS Databases
Building the Data Warehouse
Migrating to DB2
DB2: The Complete Guide to Implementation
   and Use
DB2 Design Review Guidelines
DB2: Maximizing Performance of Online
   Production Systems
Embedded SQL for DB2
SQL for DB2 and SQL/DS Application
   Developers
How to Use ORACLE SQL*PLUS
ORACLE: Building High Performance Online
   Systems
ORACLE Design Review Guidelines
Developing Client/Server Applications in an
   Architected Environment

Systems Engineering

From Mainframe to Workstations: Offloading
   Application Development
Software Configuration Management
On Time, Within Budget: Software Project
   Management Practices and Techniques
Information Systems Architecture:
   Development in the 90's
Quality Assurance for Information Systems
User-Interface Screen Design: Workstations,
   PC's, Mainframes
Managing Software Projects
The Complete Guide to Software Testing
A Structured Approach to Systems Testing
Rapid Application Prototyping
The Software Factory
Data Architecture: The Information Paradigm
Software Engineering with Formal Metrics
Using CASE Tools for Practical Management

Management

Enterprise Architecture Planning: Developing a
   Blueprint for Data, Applications, and
   Technology
Introduction to Data Security and Controls
How to Automate Your Computer Center
Controlling the Future
The UNIX Industry
Mind Your Business

IBM OS/2 Series

OS/2 Presentation Manager Programming for
   COBOL Programmers
Micro Focus Workbench for the Application
   Developer
OS/2 2.0: The Workplace Shell—A User's
   Guide and Tutorial

IBM Mainframe Series

VSE/SP and VSE/ESA: A Guide to
   Performance Tuning
CICS: A Guide to Application Debugging
CICS Application and System Programming
CICS: A Guide To Performance Tuning
MVS COBOL II Power Programmer's Desk
   Reference
VSE JCL and Subroutines for Application
   Programmers
VSE COBOL II Power Programmer's Desk
   Reference
Introduction to Cross System Product
Cross System Product Application Development
The MVS Primer
MVS/VSAM for the Application Programmer
TSO/E CLISTs: The Complete Tutorial and
   Desk Reference
CICS: A How-To for COBOL Programmers
QMF: How to Use Query Management Facility
   with DB2 and SQL/DS
DOS/VSE JCL: Mastering Job Control
   Language
DOS/VSE: CICS Systems Programming
VSAM: Guide to Optimization and Design
MVS/JCL: Mastering Job Control Language
MVS/TSO: Mastering CLISTs
MVS/TSO: Mastering Native Mode and ISPF
REXX in the TSO Environment, 2nd Edition

Technical

Rdb/VMS: Developing the Data Warehouse
AS/400 Architecture and Planning
C Language for Programmers
AS/400: A Practical Guide to Programming and
   Operations
Bean's Index to OSF/Motif, Xt Intrinsics, and
   Xlib Documentation for OSF/Motif
   Application Programmers
VAX/VMS: Mastering DCL Commands and
   Utilities
The PC Data Handbook
UNIX C Shell Desk Reference
Designing and Implementing Ethernet Networks
The Handbook for Microcomputer Technicians
Open Systems

QED books are available at special quantity discounts for educational uses, premiums, and sales promotions. Special books, book excerpts, and instructive materials can be created to meet specific needs.

This is Only a Partial Listing. For Additional Information or a Free Catalog contact
QED Information Sciences, Inc. • P. O. Box 812070 • Wellesley, MA 02181-0013
Telephone: 800-343-4848 or 617-237-5656 or fax 617-235-0826

REXX:
Tools and Techniques

Barry K. Nirmal

QED Publishing Group
Boston • London • Toronto

The contents of pages 217–222 and 251–257 have been reprinted by permission from IBM Corporation. Pages 217–222 and 251–252 in this book have been reproduced from: *TSO Extensions (TSO/E) Version 2 REXX User's Guide* (SC-28-1882) © 1988, pages 77–80 and 146–147. Pages 253–257 in this book have been reproduced from *TSO/E Version 2 REXX Reference* (SC-28-1883-1) ©1988, 1989, pages 113, 114, and 115 (Figures 4, 5, 6).

This book is available at a special discount when you order multiple copies. For information, contact QED Publishing Group, P.O. Box 812070, Wellesley, MA 02181-0013 or phone 617-237-5656.

© 1993 QED Publishing Group
P.O. Box 812070
Wellesley, MA 02181-0013

QED Publishing Group is a division of QED Information Sciences, Inc.

Library of Congress Catalog Number: 92-11612
International Standard Book Number: 0-89435-417-5

Printed in the United States of America
93 94 95 10 9 8 7 6 5 4 3 2 1

Library of Congress Cataloging-In-Publication Data

Nirmal, Barry K., 1949–
    REXX: Tools and Techniques / Barry K. Nirmal.
        p.   cm.
    Includes index.
    ISBN 0-89435-417-5
    1. Utilities (Computer programs)   2. REXX (Computer program language)   3. Assembler language (Computer program language)
    4. COBOL (Computer program language)   I. Title.
    QA76.76.U84N57   1992
    005.4'3—dc20   92-11612
                                                    CIP

Dedicated to
my wife Gargi and our children
Rahul Kumar and Rohit Kumar
whose entry into my life has made it
like
a garden in the spring, full of blooming flowers
from
a dry, barren patch of deserted land

Contents

Foreword

Avoiding the need to "reinvent the wheel" is not a new concept. This is especially true for MVS programmers, where several user groups and publications all around the world act as clearing-houses for software routines and applications designed specifi-cally to make their life easier. This area has occupied most of my recent working life as the editor of four of Xephon's *Update* jour-nals, which hopefully keep MVS technicians informed of the lat-est developments and ideas from their fellows.

It is in this capacity that I first became acquainted with the work of Barry Nirmal, whose writings have, over the years, graced several issues of both *MVS* and *CICS Update*. In this book he goes a step further and presents a whole host of utilities which form a ready-made compendium of software to help and assist the reader and his or her colleagues in their work and to offer them an in-depth knowledge of the routines' internal workings, making it relatively simple to adapt and tailor them to the needs of individual installations.

When I first started receiving REXX routines for inclusion in *MVS Update* early in 1990, my first reaction was to redirect them to the *VM Update* team. Of course I appreciated that REXX was now part of the MVS programmer's toolkit but I hadn't given serious thought to the prospect of anyone using the facility in earnest. After all, CLISTs had fulfilled this role in the MVS world for some time now and was extremely widely used. I had also interpreted the inclusion of REXX under the SAA umbrella as being more the result of IBM internal squabbles than a genuine desire to make life simpler for MVS technicians. On reading these articles again more carefully, however, I noted an appreciation and enthusiasm for REXX, which made me take it much more seriously.

Since then, several REXX execs have been published illustrating the full potential of REXX. Similarly, this book concentrates on REXX, providing the programmer with either "ready-made" solutions to real-life problems or the framework upon which to build more complex and installation-dependent routines. Everyone will find something here, whether they are after an "off the peg" solution or the seed of an idea which they can develop into something much more substantial. Enjoy!

Steve Piggott
Editor, *MVS Update*
Xephon PLC

Preface

Just like the great Russian novelist Dostoyevsky never doubted that life is its own justification and that to love, to feel compassion, to have memories, even to suffer are better than nonexistence, I have never doubted that knowledge is its own justification. When one acquires knowledge, no matter in what field, it is worth it, even if it does not seem to bring any direct, tangible, or economic benefit. But today, because the fields of knowledge have become great in number, and the human lifespan has remained approximately the same, one has to be careful in deciding the kind of knowledge that one wants to acquire.

For example, in the software field, new computer languages come and go with astonishing rapidity, and both programming managers and programmers have to be cautious in deciding which language to use for their next project. For example, I mastered Fortran, COBOL, IBM Assembler, and PL/I during the period from 1969 to 1982. But because I have not used PL/I and Fortran since 1982, I sometimes wonder if the time I spent mastering these two languages could have been better spent learning other important topics in the computing field. But I have never doubted the wisdom of my decisions to master COBOL and Assembler. The knowledge of Assembler enables me to do things that other programmers can only dream of. And the knowledge of COBOL allows me to understand and build large commercial systems.

When REXX became available on the MVS system at my installation, I read the IBM user guide for it and became immediately fascinated with it. Having written a book on CLIST (*MVS/ TSO: Mastering CLISTs*, published by QED Publishing Group, 1990) already, it was relatively easy for me to learn this language. I started to master it and I am confident that I will not repent having spent the time and effort in mastering it. The reason is best explained by the following quotation:

> REXX, a relatively young language, is gaining huge popularity in diverse environments. Originally created for IBM's VM operating system, REXX has spread to PC-DOS, VAX, UNIX, OS/2, MVS/TSO, AS/400 and even Tandem and the Commodore Amiga. With no end in sight, REXX is likely to continue to spread across even more disparate platforms thanks to its great power, simplicity, flexibility, and naturalness. ("Best Language—REXX: A New King," by Philip H. Smith III, *Enterprise Systems Journal*, March 1992)

Smith is so enthusiastic about REXX that he concludes his excellent article by saying that REXX is truly a language for the 1990s and is either available now or will be available for any operating system. It is the beauty and elegance of REXX that motivated me to write this book.

THE PROBLEM WITH SOFTWARE

Software is key to problem solutions, but it is also a key problem. This is because many companies already have more technologies and languages than they can assimilate. They don't have enough people with the skills to utilize the technologies and languages they already have, and the schools are not producing those kinds of people, either. For example, even though REXX has been available on MVS for some time, very few people know how to utilize it. Application programmers still write a COBOL program when a short REXX exec can do the job, and writing an exec takes much less time than writing a COBOL or an Assembler program. System programmers still write Assembler code, unaware that a short REXX exec can do the job. This problem can be alleviated by the easy availability of good textbooks on the subject. For example, this book shows that you no longer have to write a COBOL program if you want to write a single record of all 9s in a sequential dataset. In Chapter 5, it also shows that you no longer have to write an Assembler program if you want to display the names of all the link-list or APF libraries.

ACKNOWLEDGMENTS

I am thankful to my wife, Gargi, for her patience, understanding, and encouragement. She has always considered my books as if they were her own creations. She is probably more proud of them than I am. She and our sons, Rahul and Rohit, deserve my thanks and appreciation because the researching and writing of this book cut into the time I had available to spend with them.

I must thank Vynetta W. Ross, Program Administrator, Copyrights, at International Business Machines Corporation, Purchase, New York, for promptly granting me permission to copy a few figures from their manuals on TSO/E REXX.

I am also thankful to Ken Domantay, the DB/2 expert, for providing me with important information. My thanks to Yahya S. Al-Dhukair, the EDP Manager at SCECO (Saudi Consolidated Electric Company) East, Dammam, Saudi Arabia, for all that he has done for me. Thanks also to Dan Denver and Raman Kapoor, the MVS system programmers at SCECO East, for their helpful attitude. My special heartfelt thanks also go to my friend, Mr. S. M. Zebuq of Al-Dabal Company, Dammam, for his helpfulness. My thanks to Hira Aggarwal of Calgary, Canada for the help, encouragement, and support he gave me.

I must also thank Edwin F. Kerr, President and Publisher of QED Publishing Group for bringing out this book. The staff at QED Publishing Group, especially Beth A. Roberts, deserve my appreciation and thanks for their professionalism and efficiency.

A NOTE ABOUT THIS BOOK

I intentionally wrote this book as an advanced book on REXX containing tools and techniques that are fully annotated. I have covered some but not all the basics of the REXX language. For example, it does not tell you such things as how long a REXX variable can be, what the mathematical operators are, and how to obtain the remainder when a number is divided by another. These and other basics are covered in the IBM publication *TSO Extensions Version 2 REXX User's Guide* (SC-28-1882) for TSO implementation of REXX, and in appropriate publications for REXX implementations on other systems. These IBM manuals should be available at your installation free of cost. You may also read *REXX in the TSO Environment* by Gabriel Gargiulo, published by QED Publishing Group, to learn these basic concepts.

Two kinds of books can be written for helping a reader master a computer language. One kind covers the syntax of all the instructions and gives details about the features of the language along with short examples, but does not have complete programs or ideas on utilizing the language to build useful utilities.

The other kind of book, into which category this book belongs, covers only some of the basics of the language but has complete, useful sample programs that are accompanied by detailed instructions for installing and using them. Such a book also gives you tips about utilizing the language features to build useful utilities and solve problems on the job. Such a book, containing practical examples accompanied by detailed explanations, is more interesting to read, especially if one has one or two IBM manuals that have the syntax of instructions and other reference material.

All programs, facilities, concepts, and techniques given in this book have been developed in my spare time and thoroughly tested to work on TSO/E and MVS systems. This was done to ensure that no mistakes of any kind remained in the final text.

I tried to make the programs in this book as easy to use as possible. What is ease of use? A software product has ease of use if you don't have to attend a class to learn the product. You shouldn't have to read a manual to use it. With the help of a person who is expert in that software, if you can learn to use it in half an hour, that software has ease of use. I believe that, like using a software product that has ease of use, this book is easy to use and read as well. Happy reading!

A REQUEST TO THE READER

If you have any comments to make regarding the usefulness of this book, or have any ideas for improving it, for example, by giving some specific programs or techniques that you have in mind or have need for, please send me a note at the following address:

> Barry K. Nirmal
> c/o QED Publishing Group
> P.O. Box 812070
> Wellesley, MA 02181-0013
> U.S.A.

Introduction

1.1. IS THIS BOOK FOR YOU?

As you read this introduction, you may be trying to decide if this book is for you and whether you should spend your own or your company's money to buy it. If you are a supervisor, administrator, or a manager of programmers and systems analysts, you may be wondering if you should purchase copies of this book for all members of your group, division, or department.

As the title of this book suggests, it is a "tools and techniques" book. It contains many tools for the computer professional. These tools are the REXX execs and the accompanying programs that solve commonly encountered problems on the job. These REXX execs are ready to run on TSO and can also be used on other platforms such as VM/CMS, OS/400, and so forth with no or little change. It also contains many tips on utilizing REXX execs. These tools, techniques, and tips will be invaluable to the REXX programmer on the job.

The emphasis in this book is on teaching people to master the REXX language. This new language was made available on MVS recently, even though it has been available on VM for a number of years. It is also available on OS/400, which runs on AS/400, the machine that has become very popular internationally for medium-sized companies. (Note: REXX execs are similar to but more powerful than CLISTs that run under TSO on MVS systems. While the CLIST language has a long history behind it, the REXX language is a relative newcomer. For mastering the CLIST language, read my book *MVS/TSO: Mastering CLISTs*, published by QED Publishing Group in 1990).

All the programs and REXX execs given in this book can be easily copied to your own datasets and executed with no or little change. Complete, step- by-step procedures for installing the programs and REXX execs and using them are also given, so that even a reader who has little experience in programming can install and use them. All the programs and REXX execs are accompanied by detailed explanations. This will help you acquire a good understanding of them, which will enable you to easily modify them to meet your unique needs on the job. These complete programs and REXX execs accompanied by detailed explanations illustrate the techniques of writing programs and REXX execs for solving problems on the job.

This book also teaches a number of programming techniques, and answers commonly asked questions related to REXX.

So, if you are a programmer, a programmer/analyst, a systems analyst, or a supervisor of programmers, programmer/analysts, or systems analysts, and you work with REXX execs or MVS/TSO, this book is definitely for you. If you are a student or an instructor and you use REXX execs or MVS/TSO at your school, college, or university, this book is also for you. If you are an engineer or a scientist and you use TSO in your day-to-day work, this book can be helpful in understanding the REXX language and in learning to write REXX execs for your unique needs.

The REXX language is a very important subject for anyone who uses MVS/TSO, VM/CMS, OS/400 on an AS/400, or OS/2 Extended Edition on a PC. The reason why REXX is available on all these platforms is that REXX is part of IBM's Systems Application Architecture (SAA). SAA is not a product. It is a definition—a set of software interfaces, conventions, and protocols that provide a framework for designing and developing applications with cross-system consistency. *So, if you learn to write REXX execs under MVS/TSO, this knowledge can be used on other systems as well, such as VM/CMS, OS/400 and OS/2.* This is because REXX is part of SAA. SAA provides a framework across these IBM computing environments:

- TSO/E in the Enterprise Systems Architecture/370
- CMS in the VM/System Product or VM/Extended Architecture
- Operating System/400 (OS/400)
- Operating System/2 (OS/2) Extended Edition

Because REXX is a powerful and versatile language and, being a part of SAA, it is available on many IBM operating systems, and because this book concentrates on teaching REXX execs, its importance to the users of IBM systems cannot be overestimated.
This is all there is to deciding whether this book is for you. If it is for you, then it is worth its weight in gold. It will not only help you master programming in REXX, but also serve as a useful reference on the subject. The sample REXX execs and programs presented are of a highly practical nature. They will give you valuable insights into the kinds of needs for which REXX execs and programs can be written. This will hopefully inspire you to write similar REXX execs and programs that meet your own unique needs and that will be suitable and relevant to your own unique environment and application.

1.2.   WHAT THIS BOOK COVERS

The first chapter, which you are reading at the moment, gives you the essential information about the book's content. It also covers some fundamental concepts about REXX execs, such as what a REXX exec is, how it is executed, where it is stored, and so on.
Chapter 2 contains many REXX execs that teach REXX programming techniques. This chapter will be beneficial to anyone who wants to master the REXX language, which is a very powerful and versatile language. For example, there is one REXX exec that allows you to issue a simple command to evaluate any formula, no matter how complex. There is another exec to determine if there are any duplicate lines in a dataset and to display such lines.
Chapter 3 contains additional REXX execs that will be useful

to both applications and systems programmers. There are execs to use REXX compound variables to process arrays, both one-dimensional and two-dimensional. There is an exec that allows you to store the names of multiple datasets on an extended ISPF edit/browse panel. You can then select any of them for edit/browse or job submit by taking the cursor to the left of the desired dataset name and entering a single character. You no longer have to enter the names of your commonly used datasets every time you want to perform an edit or browse on any one of them.

Chapter 4 discusses the application of REXX execs in building useful utilities. The first section presents an exec and a COBOL program for encrypting/decrypting the content of any sequential dataset. The second section presents a case study of developing an online system using ISPF panels, REXX execs, and COBOL programs.

Chapter 5 contains some REXX execs that will mainly interest MVS systems programmers. Among others, there is one exec to display the names of link-list libraries. There are execs to define an alias entry for a dataset name prefix and to delete an alias.

Chapter 6 answers commonly asked questions regarding advanced REXX and other programming techniques. Among other techniques, you will learn how to execute a REXX exec in a batch job, and how to add a command to the ISPF command table.

In Appendixes A, B, C, and D, some REXX reference material is presented. A summary of REXX built-in functions is given in Appendix A, and in Appendix B, examples for using most of them are given. The REXX built-in functions, being numerous and powerful, are very important to the REXX programmer; the best way to master them is through short, good examples, as given in Appendix B. In Appendixes C and D, information is given related to two TSO/E external functions that are commonly used in REXX execs, SYSVAR and LISTDSI. Information given in these appendixes will help in case you don't have your REXX reference manual handy.

1.3.   WHAT THIS BOOK DOES NOT COVER

Even though this book covers a number of fundamental concepts about REXX execs later on in this chapter, and provides descriptions of and examples for using most of the REXX built-in functions in Appendixes A and B, it does not cover all the basics of the REXX language. You must acquire sound knowledge of basic REXX concepts, and syntax of REXX instructions, if you want to master the language. For example, this book does not tell you such things as how long a REXX variable can be, what the mathematical operators are, and how to obtain the remainder when a number is divided by another.

These and other basics are covered in the IBM publication *TSO Extensions Version 2 REXX User's Guide* (SC-28-1882) for TSO implementation of REXX, and in appropriate publications for REXX implementations on other systems. You may also read *REXX in the TSO Environment* by Gabriel Gargiulo, published by QED Information Sciences, to learn these basic concepts. Whenever there is something in a REXX exec in this book that you don't understand, read the *REXX User's Guide* by IBM or Gargiulo's book. You should also refer to the IBM publication *TSO/E Version 2 REXX Reference* (SC-28-1883-1) for detailed information about various topics.

However, the useful REXX execs given in this book, which are all ready to run on TSO and are accompanied by detailed explanations, will help you master the REXX language.

This book does not teach the basics of COBOL programming. In order to understand a few COBOL programs that are in this book, one should have basic knowledge of COBOL.

1.4. HOW TO BENEFIT THE MOST FROM THIS BOOK

This book is for both the experienced and the inexperienced programmer and systems analyst, in both applications and systems programming areas. Because it is more of a reference than a text, one need not read it from cover to cover. Instead you should read what interests you.

Suppose you are a systems programmer, interested mainly in knowing how REXX execs can help you in your systems programming tasks. In this case, Chapter 5 will be of special interest to you.

If you are interested in learning how REXX execs can be used with ISPF panels to build ISPF-based online facilities, read Sections 3.11 and 3.12 in Chapter 3 and 4.2 in Chapter 4.

1.5.   CONVENTIONS USED IN THIS BOOK

Since all COBOL programs and MVS JCL are coded using only uppercase characters, whenever lowercase words are used in a program or JCL you should replace the lowercase words with appropriate, meaningful words before using the program or JCL.

REXX execs can contain lowercase words, as you can see by browsing the execs presented in this book. The command entered on the terminal or in an exec to execute an exec, a CLIST, or a TSO command can also be in lower case. However, in many situations we show the command using both uppercase and lowercase words. In such instances, you should replace the lowercase words with appropriate, meaningful words before executing that command on your terminal. For example, if the command shown is

```
TSO EX (member-name) EX
```

then the words TSO and EX should be entered as is, in upper or lower case, but you must replace "member-name" with the name of a valid PDS member in your own dataset before issuing this command. Keep in mind that this guideline does not apply to lines shown in a figure. The execs shown in the figures are ready to run, and any modification to be made to an exec before using it is described in detail in the section where that exec is presented.

1.6.   WHAT IS A REXX EXEC?

REXX stands for *R*estructured *EX*tended e*X*ecutor language. This language is versatile and powerful. Its strength lies in common programming structure, readability, and free format. This makes it a good language for beginners and general users. Yet because the REXX language has powerful functions and extensive mathematical capabilities, and can be intermixed with commands to different host environments (e.g., TSO commands when a REXX exec runs under TSO), it is also suitable for more experienced computer professionals such as applications programmers, systems analysts, and systems programmers.

We use the REXX language for writing REXX programs, which are called execs. This high-level language is different from the other high-level languages such as COBOL or PL/I in that the program written in REXX is not compiled or assembled or a load module created by using the linkage-editor prior to executing a REXX exec. A REXX exec gets executed "on the fly." It gets interpreted and executed at the same time. Any error detected during execution gets displayed on the terminal, unlike a COBOL program where errors detected during compilation are displayed at compilation time and these errors are corrected and the program link-edited before executing the load module.

To understand the concept of a REXX exec, let us consider a simple example. Suppose a TSO user with prefix Z3BKN has to delete five datasets with prefix Z3BKN every time one of his batch jobs fails before submitting that job again. Rather than issue five DELETE commands from TSO, he can save himself considerable time and typing by doing the following:

1. Allocate partitioned dataset 'Z3BKN.EXEC' with the following attributes:
    Dataset Organization: Partitioned Organization (PO)
    Record Format: Fixed Blocked
    LOGICAL RECORD LENGTH: 80
    BLOCK SIZE: 9040 or some multiple of 80
    (This allocation can be done using ISPF option 3.2 or by executing program IEFBR14 in a batch job.)
2. Create member DELFILES in this dataset by using the ISPF editor and entering the following five lines, where each line starts in column 1:

```
"Delete test.file01"
"Delete test.file02"
"delete test.file03"
"delete test.file04"
"delete test.file05"
```

(Note: The entire delete commands are enclosed within double quotation marks, but the dataset names themselves are not enclosed within single quotation marks, which means that the DELETE commands will be issued against datasets with names 'Z3BKN.TEST.FILE01', 'Z3BKN.TEST.FILE02', and so on, because Z3BKN happens to be the dataset name prefix of the TSO user executing the REXX exec. Also note that it does not matter whether you enter the lines shown above in upper or lower case. They are converted to upper case before being passed to TSO as commands.)

3. Save the dataset.
   Now, every time the jobs fails and the user has to delete the five datasets, he can simply issue one of the following commands from native mode TSO or from TSO within ISPF:

```
Exec 'Z3bkn.exec(delfiles)' exec
        or
Exec (delfiles) exec
```

Note: From the command line on any ISPF panel, the user must issue the command in upper or lower case.

```
TSO EXEC (DELFILES) EXEC
```

All these commands result in the execution of the exec contained in 'Z3BKN.EXEC(DELFILES)'. This exec causes the deletion of the five datasets contained in the exec. The real advantage of REXX execs will become more apparent when we examine more complex examples of execs in subsequent chapters.

1.7. WHY DO WE NEED REXX EXECS?

REXX execs are used for a variety of tasks by applications programmers, systems programmers, computer operators, and data control personnel. Most importantly, they are used to save the user time and effort. For example, in many situations, a TSO user has to repeatedly enter the same sequence of commands. A REXX exec or a CLIST can save the user considerable time and effort in typing the commands and waiting for each to finish before entering the next command. He or she can build a REXX exec or a CLIST and enter all the commands in it. Then all there is to do is execute the exec, which will result in the execution of the command sequence contained in the exec. The commands being discussed here are usually TSO commands, but they can also be access method commands such as VTAM commands to display the status of a logical unit or to VARY a logical unit active or inactive.

REXX execs are also used in connection with running production systems. For example, consider a regular month-end cycle of an application system that consists of several sets of JCL, each of which requires minor changes each month (for example, to the dates on control cards). An operations clerk can invoke an exec or a CLIST that will automatically make these changes without the risk of accidental changes to production JCL caused by human error. REXX execs are also used to invoke software systems such as SAS, FOCUS, PANVALET, RDMS (Report Distribution and Management System), EASYTRIEVE, and so forth. They are also indispensable when building online systems using ISPF panels.

1.8.   WHERE ARE REXX EXECS STORED?

A REXX exec can be stored in either a sequential dataset or a member of a partitioned dataset (PDS). If a partitioned dataset is used, it is recommended that all members contain only REXX execs if the dataset is allocated under DDname SYSEXEC, or that all members contain only CLISTs or REXX execs if the dataset is allocated under DDname SYSPROC.

If a dataset containing REXX execs has fixed-length records, for example, Record Format (RECFM) of Fixed Blocked (FB), Record Length (LRECL) of 80, and Block Size (BLKSIZE) of 9040, the lines in the exec should start in column 1. Also, each line should have a proper sequence number in columns 73 through 80. This happens automatically under ISPF if the edit profile is properly set up.

However, if the dataset has variable-length records, for example, record format of variable blocked (VB), logical record length of 255, and block size of 9040, then the lines in the exec should start in column 9. Also columns 1 through 8 of each line should contain a proper sequence number. This happens automatically under ISPF if the dataset is edited with the proper edit profile.

For this reason, when you copy an exec using ISPF option 3.3 from a dataset with one record format to another dataset with another record format, you may encounter problems when trying to execute the exec in the "copied to" dataset. You may get an error message. Should this happen, a slight editing of the exec in the "copied to" dataset may be necessary to make the REXX exec executable again.

1.9. HOW TO CREATE AND MODIFY REXX EXECS

Suppose you want to write a small REXX exec called MYREXX. (Or perhaps you want to copy one of the simple execs from Chapter 2 and execute it. The exec in Section 2.1 is a good choice for beginners.) The first step is to allocate a partitioned dataset (PDS) that will contain this exec. Suppose SYS2.REXX.EXEC is a production library containing REXX execs that you are authorized to execute. Then it is a good idea for you to create your own REXX dataset with the same characteristics (fixed block or variable block) as SYS2.REXX.EXEC. This will allow you to concatenate your own REXX dataset with the production REXX exec library under DDname SYSEXEC or SYSPROC. To allocate your own dataset, select option 3.2 (Utilities-Dataset) of ISPF/PDF:

- View the characteristics of your production REXX library (e.g., SYS2.REXX.EXEC) and then allocate your own REXX library with the same record format, logical record length, and block size. Suppose your TSO prefix is H4RLM. You may name this dataset 'H4RLM.EXEC'. If you want to quickly allocate your PDS without knowing the name of some other library, allocate it as fixed block, with record length of 80 and block size of 9040. The number of directory blocks, volume, and primary and secondary space required should be given reasonable values. If you need help in allocating your dataset, ask any programmer in your Information Systems (or EDP) department.
- Go to option 2 (Edit) of ISPF/PDF and create member MYREXX in the dataset you allocated. While creating this exec, you need not enter line numbers. The system will automatically assign a line number to each line you enter, provided your profile is properly set up. If the dataset is fixed block, the line numbers will appear in columns 73 through 80, and if it is variable block, in columns 1 through 8.

- Save the dataset by pressing the key assigned to the END command (commonly PF3 or PF15).
- To execute this exec, enter one of the following from the command line of any ISPF panel in upper or lower case.

```
TSO EX (MYREXX) EXEC
      or
TSO EX 'H4RLM.EXEC(MYREXX)' EXEC
```

- If you want to modify this exec, select option 2 (Edit) of ISPF and edit the member. Make any changes you want and save the changes by pressing the key assigned to the END command.

1.10.   HOW IS A REXX EXEC EXECUTED?

A REXX exec can be executed in any of the three ways described below.

1.10.1.   Explicit Form of the EXEC Command

There are several different ways to execute a REXX exec. However, any exec residing in a PDS member or in a sequential dataset can be executed using the EXEC command of TSO. For example, suppose there exists a partitioned dataset called SYS2.REXX.EXEC that has a collection of REXX execs. We can execute any member of this partitioned dataset by issuing the following TSO command:

```
TSO EXEC 'SYS2.REXX.EXEC(member-name)' EXEC
```

(Note: The word EXEC, both of them, can be abbreviated as EX.) If you omit the word EXEC at the end, the system will try to interpret the content of the dataset as a CLIST and you might get error messages. But if the dataset has the following as the first line:

```
/*********** REXX *************/
```

the EXEC command will work fine, even if you omit the word EXEC from the end of the command. The reason for this is that the first line, which has a comment with word REXX, tells the system that this file contains a REXX exec rather than a CLIST. *It is therefore recommended that the first line of every REXX exec be a comment with the word REXX anywhere in it.* If you follow this convention, it has two benefits. First, you can store your exec in a PDS that also contains CLISTs. You can then allocate this PDS under DDname SYSPROC, and implicitly execute any member of this PDS by simply entering TSO followed by member name on any ISPF panel. Second, you need not enter EXEC at the end of the explicit EXEC command used to execute it, provided the dataset name was enclosed within single quotation marks, as shown above.

Another point to note is that the name of the exec dataset need not have EXEC as the last qualifier, but it is recommended. The reason for this will become clear shortly. To illustrate this point, suppose dataset 'SYS3.TEST.FILE' is a sequential dataset containing a REXX exec. This exec can be executed by issuing the following EXEC command:

```
TSO EX 'SYS3.TEST.FILE' EX
```

And if this exec has a comment on the first line with word REXX anywhere in it, the following command will also work, as explained above:

```
TSO EX 'SYS3.TEST.FILE'
```

Suppose a TSO user with prefix RF has a PDS 'RF.EXEC'. He can execute any member of this REXX library by issuing the following command:

```
TSO EX (member-name) EXEC
```

The system will expand this into EX 'RF.EXEC(member-name)' EXEC before executing it.

And if that user has a PDS 'RF.LIB.EXEC', he can execute a member of this library by executing

```
TSO EX LIB(member-name) EX
        or
TSO EX LIB.EXEC(member-name) EX
```

The system will internally expand these commands into the following before executing it:

```
TSO EX 'RF.LIB.EXEC(member-name)' EX
```

The explicit method of executing a REXX exec is the most general, though not the most practical, method. It is most general in the sense that whether or not a dataset is allocated under DDname SYSEXEC or SYSPROC during your TSO session, you can use the explicit form of the EXEC command described above to execute it. This method is used in an exec to execute another exec, but it is not frequently used by TSO users to enter commands on the terminal because it involves a lot of typing. The two other methods of executing REXX execs described below require much less typing and are therefore more frequently used.

What happens if I omit the word EXEC from the end of the command?

Example 1: Suppose your prefix is Z1BKN. Member DELFILES of PDS 'Z1BKN.REXX.EXEC' contains a REXX exec. If you enter

```
TSO EX REXX.EXEC(DELFILES)
```

the system will respond by displaying the following, provided Z1BKN.REXX.EXEC.CLIST does not exist:

```
Dataset Z1BKN.REXX.EXEC.CLIST is not in catalog or .......
```

This is because the system tries to interpret the command entered as a command to execute a CLIST. But one of the following will execute member DELFILES of 'Z1BKN.REXX.EXEC':

```
TSO EX REXX.EXEC(DELFILES) EX
            or
TSO EX REXX(DELFILES) EX
```

Example 2: Suppose your prefix is Z1BKN. Member DELFILES of PDS 'Z1BKN.EXEC' contains a REXX exec. If you enter

```
TSO EX (DELFILES)
```

the system will respond by displaying the following if Z1BKN.CLIST does not exist:

```
Dataset Z1BKN.CLIST is not in catalog or .......
```

And if Z1BKN.CLIST exists but it does not have member DELFILES, you will receive the following message:

```
Member DELFILES not in Dataset Z1BKN.CLIST
```

This is because the system tries to interpret the command entered as a command to execute a CLIST. Suppose you entered the following:

```
TSO EX EXEC(DELFILES) EX
```

The system will display the following message, provided dataset Z1BKN.EXEC.EXEC does not exist:

```
Dataset Z1BKN.EXEC.EXEC is not in catalog or ......
```

But the following command will result in the execution of member DELFILES of 'Z1BKN.EXEC':

```
TSO EX (DELFILES) EX
```

1.10.2. Implicit Form of the EXEC Command

In this method, the user simply enters the name of the REXX exec he or she wants to execute as if it was a TSO/E command. For example, suppose partitioned dataset SYS2.PROD.EXEC is allocated under DDname SYSEXEC during a TSO user's session, and this dataset contains member FOCUS. Suppose further that none of the libraries assigned to DDname STEPLIB, or ISPLLIB, or any of the other MVS areas such as link-list libraries, contains member FOCUS. To execute member FOCUS of SYS2.PROD.EXEC, the user enters the following on native TSO screen or on TSO within ISPF panel:

```
FOCUS
```

(On the command line of any ISPF panel, one has to enter TSO
FOCUS. This is true for other TSO/E commands as well, e.g.,
LISTC, TIME, LISTDS, SUBMIT, etc.)

In this case, the system first tries to determine if FOCUS is a
TSO/E command. To do this, it will first search all the libraries
allocated to DDname STEPLIB or ISPLLIB; next it will search
other MVS areas such as link-list libraries. Failing to find member FOCUS in any of them, it will then search the libraries allocated to DDname SYSEXEC. In this example, the system will
find member FOCUS as a member in SYS2.PROD.EXEC and
will execute it. The result of execution will depend on what exec
FOCUS does.

If the user knows that FOCUS is a REXX exec, he or she can
direct the system to search the libraries allocated under SYSEXEC
and then those under SYSPROC directly without having to search
the system libraries such as STEPLIB or ISPLLIB datasets. The
user does this by using the extended implicit form of the EXEC
command as described below.

Note that libraries allocated to DDname SYSPROC are supposed to contain both CLISTs and execs. (Execs are distinguished
from CLISTs by the REXX exec identifier, explained above, which is
a comment in the first line that includes the word REXX.) Libraries
allocated to DDname SYSEXEC are supposed to contain only execs.
(Your installation might have changed the name to something other
than SYSEXEC, but this is unlikely. So, for the purpose of this book,
we will call it SYSEXEC.) When both SYSEXEC and SYSPROC are
allocated during a TSO session, the system searches SYSEXEC first
before searching SYSPROC.

1.10.3.   Extended Implicit Form of the EXEC Command

This method is the fastest and the most practical method of executing a REXX exec. In this method the user simply enters a
percent sign followed by the name of the exec to execute. For example, suppose that during a TSO user's session, partitioned dataset SYS2.PROD.EXEC is allocated under DDname SYSEXEC and
that this dataset consists of execs only. To execute member FO-

CUS of this PDS, it is sufficient to enter the following on native TSO or TSO within ISPF (commonly option 6 of ISPF):

```
%FOCUS
```

The system will first search the libraries assigned to DDname SYSEXEC and, finding member FOCUS in SYS2.PROD.EXEC in this example, will execute it. Unlike what it does when you use the implicit form of the EXEC command described in the previous section, the system no longer first searches the libraries allocated to STEPLIB or ISPLLIB and the other MVS areas such as link-list libraries. It directly searches the libraries allocated to SYSEXEC followed by those allocated to SYSPROC. This results in much faster response on the user's terminal.

But, you may ask, how can I make sure that my exec library is one of the datasets allocated to DDname SYSEXEC or SYSPROC? The answer is as follows. Suppose your prefix is Z3BKN and your exec is in partitioned dataset 'Z3BKN.EXEC'. To check whether this dataset is allocated under SYSEXEC, issue this command from the command line of any ISPF panel:

```
TSO LISTA ST H
```

This command will list the names of all the datasets that are currently allocated and the DDnames under which they are allocated. Suppose DDname SYSEXEC appears in the list but your dataset 'Z3BKN.EXEC' does not appear under SYSEXEC. Suppose you find that the following two datasets are allocated to SYSEXEC:

```
SYS2.EXEC
SYS3.EXEC
```

You can add your dataset to the SYSEXEC concatenation using one of two methods given below.

Method 1: From native TSO or TSO within ISPF, first issue this command to free DDname SYSEXEC:

```
FREE F(SYSEXEC)
```

Next, allocate the new set of datasets by executing the following command from native TSO or from TSO within ISPF:

```
ALLOC F(SYSEXEC) DA('SYS2.EXEC' 'SYS3.EXEC' EXEC) SHR
```

(If the entire command does not fit on one line of the screen, you just keep on entering it on the terminal even if the cursor goes to the second line. Even if the command appears on two lines, it will execute correctly.)

Method 2: Issue the following command from native TSO or TSO within ISPF:

```
ALLOC F(SYSEXEC) DA('SYS2.EXEC' 'SYS3.EXEC' EXEC) REUSE SHR
```

The REUSE operand lets you use an already allocated DDname without first having to free it. The SHR operand lets more than one person use the allocated datasets at the same time.

1.10.4. Specifying Values at the Time of Executing an Exec

Here is an exec that receives two numbers as input. It multiplies the two numbers and displays the result:

```
ARG NUM1 NUM2
ANSWER = NUM1 * NUM2
SAY 'The product of the two numbers is ' Answer
```

Suppose your TSO prefix is RF, and you store this exec in member MULT of 'RF.EXEC'. To execute this exec explicitly, you can issue this command:

```
TSO EX 'RF.EXEC(MULT)' '40 10' EX
```

Because of the explicit form of the EXEC command, the argument (40 10) has been enclosed within single quotation marks.

But if you execute this implicitly (or using the extended implicit form) you should not specify quotation marks, as follows:

```
TSO MULT 40 10
```

1.11. CONCATENATING REXX EXEC LIBRARIES UNDER SYSEXEC OR SYSPROC

Suppose a TSO user with prefix Z1BKN has written several execs and stored them in dataset Z1BKN.LIB.EXEC. He or she would like to be able to execute execs stored in this dataset as well as those stored in SYS1.EXEC and SYS2.EXEC, which contain execs for use by all TSO users at the installation. By concatenating these three datasets under SYSEXEC or SYSPROC, the user will be able to execute any exec using the extended implicit form of the EXEC command. This concatenation can be done either in the log-on procedure or in a CLIST, in an exec, or directly on the terminal.

Suppose the user wants to allocate datasets to SYSEXEC. He or she can create an exec called MYALLOC in Z1BKN.LIB.EXEC, which is shown in Figure 1.1. In this exec we first issue the FREE F(SYSEXEC) command to free up SYSEXEC if it is already allocated. Next, we issue the ALLOC command, which concatenates the datasets in the same order in which they appear in the list. The first comma on the first and second lines of the ALLOC command is used to separate dataset names, and the second comma indi-

```
"FREE F(SYSEXEC) "
"ALLOC F(SYSEXEC) DA('Z1BKN.LIB.EXEC', ",
                 " 'SYS2.EXEC',",
                 " 'SYS1.EXEC') SHR "
IF RC = 0 THEN
    SAY 'DATASETS HAVE BEEN ALLOCATED TO SYSEXEC.'
ELSE
    SAY 'ALLOCATION TO SYSEXEC FAILED FOR SOME REASON.'
```

Figure 1.1. A sample exec that reallocates three datasets to DDname SYSEXEC.

cates that the command is continued on the next line. The single quotation marks are needed to make the dataset names fully qualified. Without the single quotation marks, TSO would append the TSO user's prefix at the beginning of the dataset name before doing the allocation. Each line is enclosed within double quotation marks because it is part of a TSO command. This is a convention of REXX execs. *All TSO commands should be enclosed within double quotation marks to distinguish them from REXX instructions.* The disposition of SHR permits these datasets to be concurrently used by other users.

Note: If the user wants to do this allocation on the terminal, he or she can first enter the following to free up SYSEXEC:

```
FREE F(SYSEXEC)
```

Next the user issues the ALLOC command directly on the terminal. To do this, he or she should enter the following command continuously, without using the double quotation marks or the line continuation characters (commas), but separating the dataset names by at least one space, or with a comma, as shown:

```
ALLOC F(SYSEXEC)
DA(LIB.EXEC,'SYS2.EXEC','SYS1.EXEC') SHR
```

Now the user can execute MYALLOC by entering the following:

```
EX LIB.EXEC(MYALLOC) EX
```

If the allocation was successful, the user should receive the following message on the terminal:

```
DATASETS HAVE BEEN ALLOCATED TO SYSEXEC.
```

1.12.   RULES FOR CONCATENATING DATASETS UNDER SYSEXEC OR SYSPROC

1. Datasets being concatenated must be either all sequential or all partitioned.
2. Datasets being concatenated must have the same record type, that is, either all with fixed-length records or all with variable-length records.

3. The order of datasets appearing in the ALLOC command or in the JCL under DDname SYSEXEC or SYSPROC is important, because the concatenation order determines the order in which TSO searches the datasets for the specified exec. Hence, the most frequently used dataset should appear first in the concatenation order.
4. The block sizes of datasets also determine the concatenation order. Where the block sizes vary, the MVS/370 (not MVS/ XA) system requires that the dataset with the largest block size appear first in the concatenation order. This is true for the ALLOC command used in a CLIST, in an exec, or directly on a terminal as well as for DDname SYSEXEC or SYSPROC appearing in the log-on procedure.

1.13.   THINGS TO REMEMBER WHEN COPYING EXECS FROM ONE DATASET TO ANOTHER

If you copy an exec from a dataset with fixed-block records into another with variable-block records using ISPF 3.3, the line numbers in columns 73–80, if they exist, will also get copied. These line numbers should be removed from columns 73–80 of the variable-blocked dataset in order to make the exec in the variable-blocked dataset executable. You can remove the line numbers using ISPF Edit (option 2).

Similarly, when you copy an exec from a dataset with variable-blocked records into another with fixed-blocked records using ISPF 3.3, the line numbers in columns 1–8 of the source dataset, if they exist, will also get copied. (When you edit a variable-blocked dataset, you normally do not see the line numbers in columns 1–8.) These line numbers should be removed from columns 1–8 of the fixed-blocked dataset in order to make the exec executable. Again, you can do this removal using ISPF Edit.

2

Some Useful REXX Execs and Facilities for Everyone

In this chapter, a number of useful REXX execs and accompanying programs are presented. These should be useful to everyone, that is, both applications and systems programmers as well as other users of the system. All the execs and programs presented in this chapter have been successfully tested on a TSO/E system. They have also been found to be really useful to the author in his day-to-day work as a systems analyst and systems programmer.

2.1. AN EXEC TO DISPLAY INFORMATION SUCH AS JULIAN DATE, USER ID, AND LOG-ON PROCEDURE NAME

Figure 2.1 shows a REXX exec that can be used to obtain important information such as user ID, Julian date, and so forth. If this exec is stored as member SYSINF in a PDS allocated to DDname SYSPROC or SYSEXEC during your TSO session, you can execute it from any ISPF panel by entering the following on the command line:

```
TSO %SYSINF
```

This exec will display a number of message lines. One such display is shown in Figure 2.2. On line 4 in this exec we are using

```
  ***********************************************************************
1 /*************** REXX ***************************************************/
2 /* Store this exec in member SYSINF of your REXX EXEC library.        */
3 /*********************************************************************/
4 user = sysvar(sysuid)
5 pref = sysvar(syspref)
6 logon_proc = sysvar(sysproc)
7 date_normal = date()
8 date_julian = date('J')
9 curr_time = time()
10 ispf = sysvar(sysispf)
11 env = sysvar(sysenv)
12 Say 'Your TSO user ID is =========>' user
13 Say 'Your prefix as defined in the user profile is ====>' pref
14 Say 'Your logon procedure name is =============>' logon_proc
15 Say 'The current date is ===============>' date_normal
16 Say 'The current date in the Julian format (yyddd) is ===>' date_julian
17 Say 'The current time is ===========>' curr_time
18 Say 'Whether ISPF dialog manager services are available '
19 Say 'for the exec (ACTIVE or NOT ACTIVE) =========>' ispf
20 Say 'Whether this exec is running in the foreground or the'
21 Say 'background (FORE = Foreground, BACK = Background) ==>' env
  ***********************************************************************
```

Figure 2.1. An exec to display important information.

```
Your TSO user ID is ===================================> Z1NMN
Your prefix as defined in the user profile is =======> Z1NMN
Your logon procedure name is ========================> @LGNZ1
The current date is =================================> 11 SEP 1991
The current date in the Julian format (yyddd) is ===> 91254
The current time is =================================> 10:44:20
Whether ISPF dialog manager services are available
for the exec (ACTIVE or NOT ACTIVE) =================> ACTIVE
Whether this exec is running in the foreground or the
background (FORE = Foreground, BACK = Background) ==> FORE
```

Figure 2.2.   One example of the messages displayed by executing the exec of Figure 2.1.

the sysvar function, which is a TSO/E external function. Option sysuid is used to obtain the user ID of the user executing this exec and store it in variable user. On line 5 we are using the sysvar function with the syspref option to obtain the prefix of the user. On line 7 we use the date function to obtain current date in the normal format. All these functions are documented in the IBM manual *TSO Extensions Version 2 REXX User's Guide* (SC-28-1882). On lines 12 through 21, we use the Say instruction to display the values of various variables on the terminal.

How can this exec be useful to IS professionals? This exec can be very helpful especially in displaying the current Julian date. Of course, the current date (in YY/MM/DD format) and time can be easily obtained by issuing the TSO command TIME. But the TIME command does not display the current date in the Julian format. Very often programmers and system analysts do not have a calendar on their desks that shows the current date in Julian. You will agree that the Julian format is used in many system displays. For example, when you issue the LISTCAT command to display information about a dataset, its creation date is shown in the Julian format. So, you can use this exec to get a rough idea of the date of creation of that dataset. What would be really desirable is to have an exec that could accept a Julian date as input, convert it into the YY/MM/DD format, and display the result. This exec should be also able to accept a date in the YY/MM/DD format and convert it into the Julian format. If you have a date conversion routine, commonly written in Assembler, available at your installation, you can easily write a REXX exec that does the date conversion described above by calling that date routine.

The exec of Figure 2.1 also shows the technique of figuring out in an exec whether ISPF dialog management services are available to the exec. If you execute a REXX exec, not from an ISPF panel or from TSO within ISPF but from the native mode of TSO, ISPF dialog management services would not be available. You can test for the availability of ISPF services before issuing commands that request ISPF services. Similarly, this exec also shows how to figure out whether your exec is running in the background or in the foreground. In Sections 6.2 and 6.3 of Chapter 6 we show how to execute a REXX exec in a batch job. If your REXX exec is running in the background, that is, in a batch job, the value assigned to env will be BACK, when you issue this instruction:

```
env = sysvar(sysenv)
```

2.2.   AN EXEC TO DELETE MULTIPLE DASD DATASETS

Figure 2.3 contains a REXX exec that shows how to delete multiple DASD datasets through an exec. Read the comments in this exec. This exec deletes six datasets whose names are given on the delete commands. Suppose the prefix of the user executing this exec is Z1ABC. The first delete command will delete the following dataset:

```
Z1ABC.PDS.CNTL
```

The next five delete commands will delete five generations of a GDG, whose base is PAYROLL.TIMECNTL.MTHBKUP.

```
/****************** REXX ******************************************/
/* This exec will delete multuple data sets that are on DASD. The  */
/* fully-qualified name of a data set can be specified on the delete */
/* command. This is done by enclosing the data set name within single */
/* quotation marks. If you omit the single quotation marks, the      */
/* system will append your TSO prefix to the beginning of the data set*/
/* name before issuing the delete command. Here, the first data set  */
/* name is partial; the rest are fully-qualified. The five fully-     */
/* qualified data set names are those of five generations of a GDG.  */
/****************************************************************/
"delete pds.cntl "
"delete 'payroll.timecntl.mthbkup.g1106v00' "
"delete 'payroll.timecntl.mthbkup.g1105v00' "
"delete 'payroll.timecntl.mthbkup.g1104v00' "
"delete 'payroll.timecntl.mthbkup.g1103v00' "
"delete 'payroll.timecntl.mthbkup.g1102v00' "
exit
```

Figure 2.3.   An exec to delete multiple DASD datasets.

How can this exec be useful to IS professionals? Suppose you have 50 datasets that you want to delete. Rather than delete them one by one through the Data Set Utility panel (usually option 3.2) of ISPF, you can set up an exec similar to the one shown in Figure 2.3. Suppose your exec is stored in member DELDASD of a PDS that is allocated to DDname SYSPROC or SYSEXEC during your TSO session; you can execute it by issuing the following command from any ISPF panel:

```
TSO %DELDASD
```

Your exec will issue delete commands against 50 datasets. They will get deleted successfully unless an error occurs, in which case error messages would be displayed on your terminal. While your exec is working, you may read something, talk to someone, or go for a drink (soft drink only, please). You are no longer tied to the terminal, which would have been the case had you decided to use ISPF option 3.2 to delete those 50 datasets.

2.3. AN EXEC TO UNCATALOG MULTIPLE TAPE DATASETS

Figure 2.4 contains a REXX exec that shows how to uncatalog through an exec multiple datasets that are on tape or cartridge. Read the comments in this exec. The first two delete commands in this exec uncatalog two generations of a GDG. These two datasets supposedly reside on tape or cartridge. Note how we use the nscr (no scratch) option on the delete commands. The nscr option tells the system to delete the entry specified on the delete command from the MVS catalog only, and not worry about scratching it from the device where it might exist. The third delete command deletes the base of the GDG from the catalog.

How can this exec be useful to IS professionals? Suppose you have 40 tape or cartridge datasets that you want to uncatalog. Rather than uncatalog them one by one through the Data Set Utility panel (usually option 3.2) of ISPF, you can set up an exec similar to the one shown in Figure 2.4. Suppose your exec is stored in member UNCAT of a PDS that is allocated to DDname SYSPROC

```
/***************** REXX *******************************************/
/* This exec will uncatalog multiple fully-qualified data sets that  */
/* reside on tape or cartridge. Finally it will delete the GDG base. */
/* If you remove single quotes from the delete command, system will  */
/* add your tso data set name prefix to the beginning of the data set */
/* name specified on the delete command.                             */
/*****************************************************************/
"delete 'payroll.tsheet.sumbkup.g1989v00' nscr "
"delete 'payroll.tsheet.sumbkup.g1990v00' nscr "
"delete 'payroll.tsheet.sumbkup' "
exit
```

Figure 2.4.   An exec to uncatalog multiple tape datasets.

or SYSEXEC during your TSO session; you can execute it by issuing the following command from any ISPF panel:

```
TSO %UNCAT
```

Your exec will issue delete commands (with nscr option) against 40 datasets. They will be uncataloged successfully unless an error occurs, in which case error messages would be displayed on your terminal. While your exec is working, you may read something, talk to someone, or go for a drink. You are no longer tied to the terminal, which would have been the case had you decided to use ISPF option 3.2 to uncatalog those 40 datasets.

2.4. AN EXEC TO RENAME MULTIPLE DASD DATASETS

Figure 2.5 contains a REXX exec that shows how to rename multiple DASD datasets through an exec. Read the comments in this exec. This exec renames three datasets whose names are given on the rename commands. Then it deletes the GDG base by issuing the delete command. (Note: TSO rename command cannot be used to rename a dataset that resides on tape or cartridge. Such a dataset should first be copied to DASD or tape under a different name, if necessary, and then uncataloged.)

How can this exec be useful to IS professionals? Suppose you have 60 DASD datasets that you want to rename. Rather than rename them one by one through the Data Set Utility panel (usually option 3.2) of ISPF, you can set up an exec similar to the one shown in Figure 2.5. Suppose your exec is stored in member RENFILES of a PDS that is allocated to DDname SYSPROC or SYSEXEC during your TSO session; you can execute it by issuing the following command from any ISPF panel:

```
TSO %RENFILES
```

Your exec will issue rename commands against 60 datasets. They will get renamed successfully unless an error occurs, in which case error messages would be displayed on your terminal. While your

```
/****************** REXX ****************************************/
/* This exec will rename fully-qualified data set names, which are   */
/* on DASD. These data sets can be generations of a GDG. If you remove*/
/* single quotation marks from the rename command, the system will   */
/* add your tso data set name prefix to the beginning of the data set */
/* name specified on the rename command.                             */
/****************************************************************/
"Rename 'payroll.tsheet.dalybkup.gl104v00'
        'prcas.cbl.billcntl.dalybkup.gl104v00' "
"Rename 'payroll.tsheet.dalybkup.gl103v00'
        'prcas.cbl.billcntl.dalybkup.gl103v00' "
"Rename 'payroll.tsheet.dalybkup.gl102v00'
        'prcas.cbl.billcntl.dalybkup.gl102v00' "
"Delete 'payroll.tsheet.dalybkup' "
exit
```

Figure 2.5. An exec to rename multiple DASD datasets.

exec is working, you may read something, talk to someone, or go for a drink. You are no longer tied to the terminal, which would have been the case had you decided to use ISPF option 3.2 to rename those 60 datasets.

2.5.   AN EXEC THAT SERVES AS A POWERFUL CALCULATOR

In Figure 2.6 is a simple REXX exec that contains only two noncomment lines. Still, it can serve as a powerful formula calculator. Read the comments given in the beginning of this figure. To use it, store this exec in member MYCALC of a PDS that is allocated to DDname SYSPROC or SYSEXEC during your TSO session. Suppose you want to make some computation, for example, your annual savings, or your hourly overtime pay. Suppose you want to obtain the value of the following expression:

```
(15000*.083*12)/3.75
```

You can issue the following command from the command line of any ISPF panel to obtain the result:

```
TSO %MYCALC (15000*.083*12)/3.75
```

The exec will display the following on your terminal:

```
The Result is 3984.0
```

You can see that this calculator can be very useful, especially when you don't have your desk calculator handy. Most programmers, like me, usually don't keep a calculator on their desks, because most of the desk space is occupied by program listings, IBM manuals, and other documents. Since they use TSO frequently, they can compute any formula, no matter how complicated, by issuing a simple command.

It should be noted that when executing this exec, no space should be present between the characters of the expression. This is because a space will signal the end of the positional parameter

```
    /******************************************************************/
1   /****************** REXX   Author: Barry K. Nirmal  *****************/
2   /* Exec Name: MYCALC   Author: Barry K. Nirmal      */
3   /******************************************************************/
4   /* To evaluate any arithmetic expression, enter the following command */
5   /* on the command line of any ISPF panel: TSO %mycalc expression    */
6   /* Note: There should be no blanks within your expression.          */
7   /* For example, you may enter: TSO %mycalc 200*(4.5+7.8+9.3+1.5)    */
8   /* or TSO EX 'your.exec.pds(mycalc)' '200*(4.5+7.8+9.3+1.5)'       */
9   /* The result displayed by this exec for this command will be 4620.0 */
10  /******************************************************************/
11  Parse arg expr .
12  Interpret 'Say "The Result is: " ' expr
    /******************************************************************/
```

Figure 2.6.   An exec that serves as a powerful calculator.

expr passed to the exec. For example, if you executed this exec as follows:

```
TSO %mycalc 120+3 -8
```

The value of expr used in the exec will be 120+3, and the result displayed will be 123.

In this exec the INTERPRET instruction is used. Suppose we replaced the Interpret instruction with the following:

```
Say 'The Result is ' expr
```

If the user issued

```
TSO %mycalc 100*3
```

the result displayed would be

```
The Result is 100*3
```

This is because the value of variable expr at the time the Say instruction is executed is string 100*3. To force the system to evaluate the content of expr as an arithmetic expression, we must use the Interpret instruction. To learn more about this seldom used but powerful instruction, refer to the IBM manual *TSO/E Version 2 REXX Reference*. To grasp the concept of the Interpret instruction, you may insert the following line before the Interpret instruction in Figure 2.6:

```
trace int
```

This will activate tracing and all intermediate results will be displayed. Note: For ease of use, you may store this exec in member CALC rather than MYCALC of your PDS. Then to evaluate any formula you can simply enter the following on any ISPF panel (as explained above):

```
TSO CALC formula
```

2.6.   AN EXEC TO DISPLAY DUPLICATE LINES IN ANY DATASET

Suppose you have a partitioned dataset. In one member of this PDS, you have entered some information, for example, employee or customer numbers, or the names of some datasets, in columns 1 through 44 of each record. (Information starts in column 1 and ends in column 44 or earlier.) It is possible that a program created the records in this dataset. You want to know if there are any lines with duplicate information in this file. (Information here means employee or customer number, or dataset names, present in columns 1–44 of each record.)

How do you do this? Do it manually? A very bad idea, because manually checking for duplicate records is a tedious and error-prone task, if there are more than a dozen records. Write a COBOL program that will do this checking? Not a very good idea, because COBOL programs are so lengthy, take a long time to write, and need to be compiled and linked, and JCL needs to be set up before they can be executed. Perhaps write a program in SAS or Easytrieve? Not a bad idea. *But why not write a REXX exec?* A pretty good idea indeed. The REXX exec that solves this problem is shown in Figure 2.7. Read the comments in this figure now before proceeding further.

Procedure for installing this exec

Step 1. Copy the content of Figure 2.7 in member DUPDSN of a PDS that is allocated to DDname SYSPROC or SYSEXEC during your TSO session.

Step 2. On line 50, DDname SYSOUT is allocated to sysout class Q. Change Q to a class that is valid at your installation and is reserved for the TSO held class.

Step 3. Consult with your MVS systems programmer, and check that the load library containing module SORT (sort program) is present in the MVS link-list. If not, obtain the name of the sort library, and change line 51 to the following:

```
CALL 'full.name.of.load.library(SORT)'
```

```
********************************************************************
   1  /******************** REXX ********************************/
   2  /* Exec Name: DUPDSN     Author: Barry K. Nirmal          */
   3  /********************************************************** */
   4  /* This exec will prompt you for the name of a PDS, and then the name */
   5  /* of the member that contains data set names in positions 1 to 44.   */
   6  /* Member sortparm of the PDS whose name you provide must contain the  */
   7  /* following three records:                               */
   8  /* SORT FIELDS=(1,44,CH,A),EQUALS                         */
   9  /* RECORD TYPE=F                                          */
  10  /* END                                                    */
  11  /* Note: Ensure these three lines are in upper-case and start in       */
  12  /*       column 2.                                        */
  13  /* The PDS should have record length of 80, but it may have any other  */
  14  /* record length that is equal to or greater than 44. This exec will   */
  15  /* sort the records on sort field equal to first 44 bytes of records.  */
  16  /* It will then read the sorted file, and compare the first 44 bytes   */
  17  /* of the current record with the first 44 bytes of the previous one.  */
  18  /* If they are the same, it will inform you that a duplicate DSN was    */
  19  /* found. It will also inform you the record number of the record with */
  20  /* duplicate DSN in the sorted file. After the exec has ended, the      */
  21  /* sorted file will be present in member JUNK01 of your PDS. You may    */
  22  /* browse and then delete it if you wish. If you don't receive any      */
  23  /* duplicate DSN message, this means that no duplicates were found.     */
  24  /* Before terminating, it will disply the total nember of records       */
  25  /* read from the input PDS member.                        */
  26  /********************************************************** */
  27  /* This exec needs no change before running it. But make sure the       */
  28  /* first 44 characters of input records have data set name followed by */
********************************************************************
```

```
29  /* spaces, if any. This exec ignores the content of records after    */
30  /* position 44 for all purposes including sorting and comparing.      */
31  /* A record with an asterisk in position 1 is considered a comment.   */
32  /**********************************************************************/
33  pdsname = ' '
34  Do while pdsname = ' '
35    Say 'Enter the name of PDS (fully-qualified but no quotes) please:'
36    Pull pdsname
37  End
38  memname = ' '
39  Do while memname = ' '
40    Say 'Enter the name of PDS member containing DSN in positions 1-44: '
41    Pull memname
42  End
43  "Free f(sortin sortout sysin sysout sortwk01 sortwk02 sortwk03)"
44  "Alloc f(sortin)  da('"pdsname"("memname")') shr"
45  "alloc f(sortout) da('"pdsname"(junk01)') shr"
46  "alloc f(sysin) da('"pdsname"(sortparm)') shr"
47  "alloc f(sortwk01) space(1) cylinders new"
48  "alloc f(sortwk02) space(1) cylinders new"
49  "alloc f(sortwk03) space(1) cylinders new"
50  "alloc f(sysout) sysout(Q)"
51  sort
52  "free f(sysin sysout)"
53  "alloc f(sysin) da(*)"
54  "alloc f(sysout) da(*)"
55  done = 'no'
```

Figure 2.7.   An exec to display duplicate lines in any dataset. *continues*

```
56  recnum = 0
57  Prevdsn = ' '
58  DO while done = 'no'
59      "execio 1 diskr sortout "
60      if RC = 0 then
61      DO
62          pull record
63          recnum = recnum + 1
64          if substr(record,1,1) = '*' Then NOP
65          else do
66              currdsn = substr(record,1,44)
67              If currdsn = prevdsn     Then
68                  Say 'Line number ' recnum ' in sorted file has duplicate DSN'
69              ELSE nop
70              prevdsn  = currdsn
71          End
72      End
73      Else done = 'yes'
74  End
75  "Execio 0 diskr sortout (FINIS" /* Close so file can be freed */
76  "Free f(sortin sortout)"
77  Say 'Sir/Madam, Total Number of Records Processed: ' Recnum
78  Say 'The sorted file which you can browse is: 'pdsname'(JUNK01)'
79  Exit 0
*********************************************************************
```

Figure 2.7.   (Continued)

(You must replace full.name.of.load.library with the actual name of the load library that contains member SORT.)

Procedure for using this exec

Step 1. Suppose you have a PDS that has fixed-length records of length 80. (The record length can be anything so long as it is 44 or more.) In member A of this PDS you have created records that have information such as employee or customer numbers, or data-set names, in positions 1–44. In member SORTPARM of this PDS, you should enter the three sort control records, given on lines 8, 9, and 10 in Figure 2.7.

Step 2. From the command line of any ISPF panel, enter the following:

```
TSO %DUPDSN
```

The exec shown in Figure 2.7 will start executing. It will prompt you for the name of your PDS. It will then prompt you for the member name that contains records that are to be examined for duplicates. Once you have entered the member name, it will sort the records in the specified member and create a sorted file in member JUNK01 of the same PDS. It will then read the sorted file, and check for duplicates. If it does not display any duplicate record message, this means that it found no duplicates.

Explanation of the exec of Figure 2.7. Lines 1 through 32 are comments. On lines 33 through 42 it prompts the user for the PDS name and the member name. It stores these values in variables pdsname and memname. On lines 43 through 50 it allocates various ddnames required for executing the sort program. On line 51 it executes the sort program. After control comes back from the sort program, line 52 is executed. In the code that follows, we read each member of the sorted file. The execio command on line 59 reads the next record from the file allocated to DDname sortout. If end-of-file is encountered, RC will be set to nonzero. Assuming that a record was read, on line 62 we would store it in variable record. If the first character of this record is an asterisk, we would treat it as a comment and bypass it; otherwise we would store the first 44 characters of record in variable currdsn (see line 66). We would then compare currdsn with the first 44 characters of the previous record (see line 67). If the two are equal, on line 68 we would display a message indicating that a record with duplicate information was found. When end-of-file is encountered on reading file sortout, control comes to line 73 where done is set to yes, and the DO WHILE loop begun on line 58 and ended by the End on line 74 will be exited. The control will then flow to line 75 where file sortout will be closed so it can be freed. On line 76 we are freeing up two DDnames. On lines 77 and 78 we are displaying messages on the terminal. The execution of line 79 terminates this exec.

How can this exec be useful in your daily work? The exec shown in Figure 2.7 can be easily modified to suit your unique needs. Suppose you have written a program to create a sequential file that has employee numbers in positions 1–10 of each record. You want to know if this file has any duplicate employee numbers. You can use the exec of Figure 2.7 without any change, if you ensure that positions 11 through 44 of each record contain spaces only. If not, you may make the following changes to make it work properly:

1. In member SORTPARM of the PDS where your sequential file is stored as a member, make sure the first record has:

```
SORT FIELDS=(1,10,CH,A),EQUALS
```

2. Change line 40 to the following:

```
Say 'Enter the PDS member that has employee
numbers'
```

3. Change Q on line 50 to a valid class meant for TSO held output.
4. Change line 66 to the following:

```
currdsn = substr(record,1,10)
```

Now execute the modified exec. It should work correctly.

2.7. AN EXEC TO DEFINE A KEY-SEQUENCED VSAM DATASET

Figure 2.8 shows a REXX exec that can be of great help to application programmers in defining VSAM key-sequenced datasets (KSDS). Defining a VSAM dataset is an intimidating task, especially to the new programmers, because the DEFINE cluster command has many interdependencies between its parameters, and there are many technical considerations to keep in mind. So if an installation sets up a REXX exec that can be used by the new programmers to define VSAM datasets, it would help them a great deal. They can use this exec to define VSAM files and get down to the task of writing application programs, whether online or batch, that access these files. Once they have gained sufficient experience, they can take a course on VSAM that explains how to choose the parameters on DEFINE CLUSTER for optimum performance.

How does this exec work? If this exec is stored in member VSAMDEF in a PDS that is allocated under DDname SYSEXEC or SYSPROC during the user's TSO session, he or she can invoke it by entering the following command on the command line of any ISPF panel:

```
TSO %VSAMDEF
```

The user will be prompted to enter values for the various parameters needed to define the file, such as the VSAM cluster name and the record length. If the record key starts at the first position in the record, the user must enter 1 and not zero, even though the LISTCAT command displays zero as RKP (Relative Key Position) for such a file. When RKP displayed is zero, this means that the key is in position 1, that is, at offset zero from the beginning of the record. If the user entered 1 as the value for STARTPOS, the exec would subtract 1 from this value on line 30, resulting in OFFSET assuming a value of zero. On the KEYS parameter of the DEFINE CLUSTER, the value used for OFFSET would be zero, which would be correct.

After obtaining all the necessary parameters from the user, the DELETE command is issued on line 33 to delete that cluster. The DELETE command may fail if the VSAM file does not exist,

```
1    /******************* REXX *******************/
2    /* THIS EXEC IS USED TO DEFINE A VSAM KEY-SEQUENCED DATASET*/
3    /*********************************************/
4    SAY 'THIS EXEC WILL DEFINE A VSAM KSDS FOR YOU, ACCORDING TO'
5    SAY 'THE FILE PARAMETERS PROVIDED BY YOU. GOOD LUCK.'
6    SAY 'KINDLY ENTER THE FULLY-QUALIFIED VSAM CLUSTER NAME ===>'
7    SAY '(DO NOT ENTER QUOTATION MARKS, PLEASE.)'
8    PULL FILENAME
9    SAY 'ENTER ESTIMATED NUMBER OF RECORDS THIS FILE WILL CONTAIN'
10   PULL NUMREC
11   SAY 'ENTER THE LENGTH OF RECORDS THIS VSAM FILE WILL CONTAIN'
12   PULL RECSIZE
13   TOPROMPT = 'YES'
14   DO WHILE TOPROMPT = 'YES'
15     SAY 'ENTER THE KEY LENGTH PLEASE'
16     PULL KEYLEN
17     IF KEYLEN > 0 & KEYLEN < RECSIZE THEN
18       TOPROMPT = 'NO'
19     ELSE SAY 'THE KEY LENGTH MUST BE > 0 AND LESS THAN RECORD SIZE'
20   END
21   TOPROMPT = 'YES'
22   DO WHILE TOPROMPT = 'YES'
23     SAY 'AT WHAT POSITION IN THE REORD DOES THE VSAM KEY START?'
24     PULL STARTPOS
25     ENDPOS = STARTPOS + KEYLEN - 1
```

40

```
26    IF STARTPOS > 0   & ENDPOS  <=  RECSIZE THEN
27        TOPROMPT = 'NO'
28        ELSE SAY 'START POSITION AND END POSITION NOT WITHIN RECORD'
29    END
30    OFFSET = STARTPOS - 1
31    SAY 'ENTER THE DASD VOLUME WHERE THIS FILE IS TO BE DEFINED'
32    PULL VOLSER
33    "DELETE '"FILENAME"' "
34    "DEFINE CLUSTER (NAME ('"FILENAME"') RECORDS("NUMREC")",
35        " SHR(2 3) VOLUME("VOLSER") RECSZ("RECSIZE" "RECSIZE")",
36        " CISZ(2048) FREESPACE(10 10) KEYS("KEYLEN" "OFFSET"))",
37        " DATA(NAME('"FILENAME".D'))",
38        " INDEX(NAME('"FILENAME".I'))"
39    IF RC = 0 THEN
40        SAY 'SIR/MADAM, THE VSAM FILE HAS BEEN SUCCESSFULLY DEFINED.'
41    ELSE
42        DO
43            SAY 'AN ERROR OCCURRED ON DEFINE CLUSTER COMMAND'
44            SAY 'FIND OUT THE CAUSE OF THE ERROR AND TRY AGAIN'
45            EXIT
46        END
47    SAY 'DO YOU WANT THIS FILE LOADED WITH A RECORD WHOSE KEY'
```

Figure 2.8.   A REXX exec to define a key-sequenced VSAM file and load it with a record containing 9 in all key positions.

continues

```
48   SAY 'CONTAINS 9 IN ALL POSITIONS (Y/N)?'
49   PULL ANS
50   IF ANS = 'Y' THEN
51     DO
52       "ALLOCATE F(INPUT) DA('SYS3.PARMLIB(VSAM9999)') SHR"
53       "ALLOC F(OUTPUT) DA('"FILENAME"') SHR"
54       "REPRO INFILE(INPUT) OUTFILE(OUTPUT)"
55       SAY 'SIR/MADAM, THIS FILE HAS BEEN LOADED WITH ONE RECORD.'
56     END
57   SAY 'GOOD BYE MY DEAR USER.....HAVE A GOOD DAY.........'
58   EXIT
```

Figure 2.8.   (Continued)

but it would not prevent the exec from proceeding to the next line where the DEFINE CLUSTER command is issued. DELETE and DEFINE CLUSTER are Access Method Services (AMS) commands that are processed by the Access Method Services program (IDCAMS) that is used to define and maintain VSAM datasets, MVS catalogs, and so forth. The AMS commands are described in detail in this (or an equivalent) IBM publication: *MVS/Extended Architecture Access Method Services Reference* (GC-26-4135).

If an error occurred in executing the DEFINE CLUSTER command, control would go to line 43 where two message lines would be displayed, followed by the execution of the EXIT instruction on line 45. The EXIT instruction would terminate the exec. If the DEFINE CLUSTER ended successfully, line 40 would be executed where the user would be informed. Next, the user is prompted to indicate whether he or she wants a record containing 9 in key positions loaded to this file. This is recommended if the file is to be subsequently opened by a batch program or CICS. The user may not want such a record loaded if he or she wants to load this VSAM file from a sequential file containing one or more records.

If the user enters Y in response to the query on lines 47 and 48, the exec attempts to allocate under DDname INPUT the dataset 'SYS3.PARMLIB(VSAM9999)' whose record length must be less than or equal to the record length of the VSAM file. This file supposedly contains only one record with 9 in all positions. On line 53 the VSAM file is allocated under DDname OUTPUT, which is followed by the REPRO command of AMS. This command copies all records (actually only one record in this example) from the file allocated under DDname INPUT to the file allocated under DDname OUTPUT. On line 57, we display the goodbye message. The EXIT instruction on line 58 terminates the exec, sending control back to TSO.

2.8.   AN EXEC TO SUBMIT A JOB AFTER CHANGING ONE LINE IN IT

Here is a REXX technique that can be of great help to you, whether you are in systems or applications programming. To illustrate this technique, let us take an example. Suppose Bill is a CICS systems programmer, responsible for managing 10 CICS regions. He often has to modify the procedures for starting the various CICS regions. Suppose he has modified CICSPRD1, the startup procedure for the first CICS production region, in SYS2.PROCLIB. Bill now wants to check if that procedure has any syntax errors. What Bill normally does is edit the dataset containing the job shown in Figure 2.9. (Suppose this job is stored in member PROCSCAN in Bill's dataset 'prefix.JOBS.CNTL' where the prefix is Bill's TSO prefix. Let's say Bill's prefix is Z1BKN.) He ensures that the first line in this job contains a valid JOB statement. He then changes CICSXXXX on the last line to CICSPRD1 and submits the job. If TSO notification indicated that the job ended without any JCL error, he would know that procedure CICSPRD1 that he had modified contained no syntax errors. (It could still contain some other kind of JCL error, e.g., a dataset specified in the JCL not being cataloged.)

Suppose that ten minutes later, Bill had to modify member CICSPRD2 in SYS2.PROCLIB. He would follow the same procedure described above to verify that procedure CICSPRD2 contained no syntax errors. But Bill can work smart, thanks to the power of REXX that is at his disposal. He can write a REXX exec that would edit the dataset shown in Figure 2.9, make the change, and submit the job. This would save Bill a lot of time and effort, and would also be less error-prone. No longer does Bill have to manually edit the dataset, issue the SUBMIT command, press the END key to terminate edit, and wait for system response after each and every command. The REXX exec that Bill can use is shown in Figure 2.10.

How Does This Exec Work? If this exec is stored in member SCANJ in a PDS that is allocated to DDname SYSEXEC or SYSPROC during Bill's TSO session, and he wanted to check procedure CICSPRD1 for syntax errors, all that Bill must do is issue this command from the command line of any ISPF panel:

```
TSO %SCANJ PRD1
```

This exec would submit the job shown in Figure 2.9 after changing the last line from CICSXXXX to CICSPRD1. It would then end the

```
//jobname JOB Statement Goes Here
//*********************************************************
//* THIS JOB WILL SCAN A PROCEDURE STORED IN SYS2.PROCLIB
//* FOR SYNTAX ERRORS. MAKE SURE THIS JOB HAS TYPRUN=SCAN
//* OPERAND ON THE JOB STATEMENT.
//*********************************************************
//STEP01 EXEC CICSXXXX
```

Figure 2.9. The batch job that is modified and then submitted by the exec of Figure 2.10.

EDIT command without saving the changes made to the job. This is necessary because the next time this exec is invoked, it would try to change string CICSXXXX. Therefore in order for this exec to work, the dataset containing the job of Figure 2.9 must always contain a valid JOB statement with TYPRUN=SCAN, and CICSXXXX on the EXEC statement.

```
01  /****************** REXX *********************
02  ARG USERDATA
03  LEN = LENGTH(USERDATA)
04  CICSNAME = 'CICS'
05  CICSNAME = INSERT(USERDATA,CICSNAME,4,LEN)
06  QUEUE "CHANGE * 100 'CICSXXXX' '"CICSNAME"' ALL"
07  QUEUE "SUBMIT"
08  QUEUE "END NOSAVE"
09  "EDIT 'Z1BKN.JOBS.CNTL(PROCSCAN)' NONUM OLD DATA"
10  EXIT
```

Figure 2.10. A REXX exec that automates the function of submitting the batch job shown in Figure 2.9.

This exec is quite straightforward. Let us say the user enters the following:

```
TSO SCANJ PRD4
```

On line 2 variable USERDATA is assigned the value PRD4. On line 3 variable LEN is assigned the value 4, because the length of USERDATA is 4. On line 4 variable CICSNAME is assigned the value 'CICS'. On line 5 the INSERT function is used to insert the content of USERDATA in string CICSNAME after leaving four characters from the beginning. Therefore, after line 5 has executed, the value of CICSNAME in this example would be CICSPRD4. On lines 6, 7, and 8 we use the QUEUE instruction to insert three lines on the data stack. These lines are actually subcommands of EDIT. On line 9 we issue the EDIT command to edit dataset 'Z1BKN.JOBS.CNTL(PROCSCAN)'. This dataset is supposed to contain the JCL shown in Figure 2.9. The EDIT command will cause the stack to be searched for the subcommands. First the CHANGE subcommand will be fetched and executed. The CHANGE subcommand of EDIT on line 6 indicates that 100 lines from where the current line pointer is positioned are to be scanned, and all occurrences of string CICSXXXX are to be changed to CICSnnnn where nnnn is the four-character string passed to this exec by the user. (The asterisk following the word CHANGE indicates the line where the current line pointer is pointing, which in this exec would be the top of the dataset being edited.) In this example, 100 lines from the top of the dataset would be scanned for string CICSXXXX and all occurrences of this string would be changed to CICSPRD4. Since this dataset contains far less than 100 lines, specifying 100 ensures that all lines in the dataset are covered. Next, the SUBMIT subcommand would be fetched from the stack. This would cause the content of the dataset being edited to be submitted as a batch job. Next, the END NOSAVE subcommand would cause the EDIT command to terminate. The changes made to the dataset would not be saved.

Remember that when an exec issues a PULL instruction, or when it issues an interactive TSO/E command such as EDIT and LISTDS, the data stack is searched first for information and, if that is empty, information is fetched from the terminal.

2.9. AN EXEC TO SUBMIT A COMPILE AND LINK JCL AFTER INSERTING CORRECT PROGRAM ID EVERYWHERE

Suppose that dataset prefix.RESYS.SRCE(JCLB1) contains a JCL that you use to compile and link a program, where prefix stands for your TSO prefix. If you want to compile and link program P1, you can edit this dataset, insert P1 as the program ID on all lines that refer to program ID, and then submit the JCL. This is definitely a time-consuming process, especially if you submit compile and link jobs frequently. A better method, which involves less manual work, is as follows:

- Change prefix.RESYS.SREC(JCLB1) so that it has string 12345678 as program ID on all lines where necessary.
- Copy the exec shown in Figure 2.11 in member $JCL of a PDS that is allocated to DDname SYSEXEC or SYSPROC during your TSO session.
- Allocate sequential dataset prefix.W1 with record length of 80. It will be used by the REXX exec as a work file.

Now, if you want to submit the compile and link JCL for program P1, you can simply issue the following from the command line of any ISPF panel:

```
TSO $JCL P1
```

And, if you wanted to submit the compile and link JCL for program PAYCOMP1, you would issue the following command:

```
TSO $JCL PAYCOMP1
```

Now suppose you wanted to submit the compile and link jobs for 100 programs. It would be a pain to manually issue 100 commands. You can automate this process as follows. Enter the IDs of 100 programs in a 80-byte sequential dataset, with one program ID on each line. Let us call it control file. Next write a REXX exec by modifying the one shown in Figure 2.11 so that it reads one record from the control file, obtains the program ID, modifies the compile and link JCL to change string 12345678 to

```
   /***********************************************************/
   /****************** REXX *****************************************/
1  /*******************************************************************/
2  /* AUTHOR: Barry K. Nirmal                                      */
3  /* Store this exec in member $JCL of a PDS allocated to SYSEXEC. */
4  /*******************************************************************/
5  /* The string to be changed in the input file must be '12345678' and */
6  /* It must be 8 bytes long. The target string can be 1 to 8 bytes    */
7  /* long.                                                             */
8  /*******************************************************************/
9  arg pgm .
10 pgm = strip(pgm,'T')
11 If length(pgm) > 8 | length(pgm) = 0 then
12 DO
13    say 'program name ' pgm ' is longer than 8 bytes or it is null.'
14    say 'This exec is abnormally terminating'
15    exit
16 END
17 "Alloc F(refjcl) DA(resys.srce(jclbl)) shr reuse"
18 "Alloc F(newjcl) DA(wl) shr reuse"
19 queue pgm
20 Call Subjcl
21 exit 0
```

```
22  /***********************************************************/
23  /* The following is an internal subroutine. If you wish, you may make */
24  /* it an external subroutine, in which case it can be called by more  */
25  /* than one exec. The calling exec can allocate a different dataset   */
26  /* to DDname REFJCL before calling the external subroutine SUBJCL.    */
27  /***********************************************************/
28  SUBJCL:
29  Pull pgm
30  done = 'no'
31  do while done = 'no'
32    "Execio 1 diskr refjcl"
33    if RC = 0 then
34    do
35      pull record
36      Loc = index(record,'12345678')
37      If loc ¬= 0 Then
38      do
39        record = overlay(pgm,record,loc.8)
40        myloc = loc + length(pgm)
41        endloc = loc + 8
42        charl = substr(record,endloc,1)
43        if charl \= ' ' & length(pgm) < 8 Then
44        do
```

Figure 2.11. An exec to submit a compile and link JCL after making global changes.

continues

```
45          record = overlay(char1,record,myloc,1)
46          record = overlay(' ',record,endloc,1)
47      end
48    else NOP
49    end
50  Else NOP
51    push record
52    "Execio 1 Diskw newjcl"
53      end
54    Else done = 'yes'
55  end
56  "Execio 0 diskw newjcl   (FINIS"
57  "execio 0 diskr refjcl  (FINIS"
58  "Submit w1"
59  Say 'Sir/Madam, the job for program ' pgm ' has been submitted'
60  Return
*****************************************************************************
```

Figure 2.11. (Continued)

50

this program ID, and submits the job. It then reads the next record from the control file and repeats the process. This way it would submit 100 jobs. If you did this, you would have to issue just one command, and the exec would do the rest. This is how smart programmers and analysts work.

The concept given above is applicable not only to compile and link jobs but to any job that needs to be modified before being submitted.

2.10. AN EXEC TO INVOKE ISPF BROWSE FROM ANY ISPF PANEL

Suppose your prefix is Z1ABC and your dataset Z1ABC.ADDR.TEL is a sequential dataset containing names, addresses, and telephone numbers of all your friends and business contacts. Rather than store addresses and telephone numbers in a paper file, you have decided to store them in a dataset. This allows you to easily add, delete, or change records in the dataset using the power of ISPF Edit. Whenever you want to contact a person, you browse this dataset and use the FIND command to find his or her address and/or telephone numbers. This is faster than checking a diary or a paper file, especially if you have to browse this dataset on a frequent basis during the course of a working day. You can, of course, select the browse option (normally option 1) of TSO/ISPF and, when the browse entry panel is displayed, you must enter the name of this dataset and press the Enter key. The browse panel with the first few records from this dataset will then be displayed.

The other alternative is to write a REXX exec that can be invoked from any ISPF panel as a TSO command. This exec is shown in Figure 2.12. This three-line exec can be of immense help to you. If it is stored in member ADRTEL in a partitioned dataset that is allocated either to DDname SYSEXEC or to SYSPROC during your TSO session, all you must do is issue the TSO command %ADRTEL on the command line of any ISP panel. The system will immediately display the browse panel containing the first few records from dataset 'prefix.ADDR.TEL' where prefix will be replaced by your TSO prefix. When you press the PF key assigned to the END command (normally PF3 or PF15) to terminate browse,

```
/*********** REXX *************/
"ISPEXEC BROWSE DATASET(ADDR.TEL)"
EXIT
```

Figure 2.12.   An exec to invoke ISPF Browse from any ISPF panel.

you will be returned to the panel where the command %ADRTEL was issued.

The above REXX exec uses command ISPEXEC. It is part of ISPF (Interactive System Productivity Facility), which allows you to develop interactive applications using REXX execs, panels, messages, tables, and so forth. (We will not discuss in any great detail in this book the techniques of developing online applications using ISPF panels, because it is not a small topic and requires a separate volume to properly teach all the concepts and techniques involved. However, in Section 4.2 of Chapter 4 you will find a case study for developing an online system called "Programmer's Toolbox" using ISPF panels, REXX execs, and a COBOL program. A good understanding of the material presented in that section will enable you to quickly build online systems that meet your day-to-day needs.)

If you or your users frequently browse a dataset, for example, one containing information about all the IBM manuals available in your department library, you may set up an exec similar to the one given above and execute that exec, rather than go through the browse panel of ISPF. The savings in time and effort will be significant, as you can easily verify yourself.

The ISPEXEC command with the BROWSE option can also be used to allow a TSO user who does not have access to the entire ISPF facility, or who does not have knowledge about using ISPF (e.g., a data control clerk), to browse selected datasets. It should be noted that under TSO, an MVS installation can be running many applications such as ISPF, FOCUS, and DB2. Not all TSO users will be able to access all the applications running under TSO when they log onto TSO. The technique of using CLISTs (REXX execs can be used in the place of CLISTs) to restrict TSO users' access to applications running under TSO is discussed in my book *MVS/TSO: Mastering CLISTs*.

2.11.   AN EXEC TO INVOKE ISPF EDIT FROM ANY ISPF PANEL

Suppose you frequently edit a dataset, which can be sequential or partitioned. The dataset name, for example, is

```
'BILLING.PDS.CNTL(USERS)'
```

You want a facility so that you can invoke ISPF Edit for this dataset while you are on any of the ISPF panels, and then return to the original panel. The REXX exec shown in Figure 2.13 will do this job for you.

This exec can be stored in any PDS that is allocated under DDanme SYSEXEC or SYSPROC, for example, under name EDTUSR. Then from the command line of any ISPF panel, you can invoke it by entering this command:

```
TSO %EDTUSR
```

This exec will display the edit panel for the dataset, bypassing the edit entry panel. After you have finished editing the dataset, and press the PF key assigned to the END command (normally PF3 or PF15), you will be returned to the panel where you issued the %EDTUSR command.

As you can see, the time saved from using this REXX exec is significant. The ISPEXEC command used in this and the previous section is fully described in the IBM manual *Interactive System Productivity Facility (ISPF) Dialog Management Services* (SC-34-2088).

```
/*********** REXX *************/
"ISPEXEC EDIT DATASET('BILLING.PDS.CNTL(USERS)')"
EXIT
```

Figure 2.13.   An exec to invoke ISPF Edit from any ISPF panel.

2.12. AN EXEC TO CONVERT A DECIMAL NUMBER INTO HEXADECIMAL

Figure 2.14 shows a small REXX exec that can be used to convert any decimal number (without fractions) into its hexadecimal representation. Read the comments in this exec. If this exec is stored in member GIVEHEX in a PDS that is allocated to DDname SYSPROC or SYSEXEC during your TSO session, you can enter the following on the command line of any ISPF panel to convert decimal number 1005, for example, into hexadecimal:

```
TSO %GIVEHEX 1005
```

This exec receives the positional parameter passed to it in variable dec (see the first noncomment line in Figure 2.14). On the next line, we are using the d2x function of REXX to convert the content of variable dec into hexadecimal and store the result in variable hex. On the next line we display the values of variables dec and hex along with some text to make the message easy to read.

2.13. AN EXEC TO CONVERT A HEXADECIMAL NUMBER INTO DECIMAL

Figure 2.15 shows a small REXX exec that can be used to convert any hexadecimal number into its decimal representation. Read the comments in this exec. If this exec is stored in member GIVEDEC in a PDS that is allocated to DDname SYSPROC or SYSEXEC during your TSO session, you can enter the following on the command line of any ISPF panel to convert hexadecimal number 100A, for example, into its decimal equivalent:

```
TSO %GIVEDEC 100A
```

This exec receives the positional parameter passed to it in variable HEX (see line 8 in Figure 2.15). On line 9 we are using the x2d function of REXX to convert the content of variable HEX into decimal and store the result in variable DEC. On line 10 we display the values of variables HEX and DEC, along with some text to make the message easy to read.

```
********************************************************************
1  /********************* REXX ********************************/
2  /* Exec Name: GIVEHEX    Author: Barry K. Nirmal          */
3  /* For example, if you enter on any ISPF panel: TSO GIVEHEX 100 */
4  /* The result displayed will be the following:            */
5  /* Decimal  100 = Hexadecimal  64                          */
6  /**********************************************************/
7  arg dec .
8  hex = d2x(dec)
9  Say 'Decimal ' dec ' = Hexadecimal ' hex
********************************************************************
```

Figure 2.14. An exec to convert a decimal number into hexadecimal.

55

```
   ******************************************************************
1  /****************** REXX ****************************************/
2  /* Exec Name: GIVEDEC    Author: Barry K. Nirmal                */
3  /**************************************************************/
4  /* For example, if you enter on any ISPF panel: TSO GIVEDEC 100 */
5  /* The result displayed by this exec for this command will be:  */
6  /* Hexadecimal  100  = Decimal  256                             */
7  /**************************************************************/
8  arg hex .
9  dec = x2d(hex)
10 Say 'Hexadecimal ' hex ' = Decimal ' dec
   ******************************************************************
```

Figure 2.15. An exec to convert a hexadecimal number into decimal.

2.14.   AN EXEC TO DISPLAY ALL LINES IN A DATASET THAT CONTAIN A SPECIFIED STRING

In Figure 2.16 is an exec that shows how to read a dataset sequentially from the first record to the last. Suppose you have a dataset and you want to know if it contains string COND. You want to see all the records that contain this string. This exec will do this job for you. If it is stored in member SCANSEQ in a PDS that is allocated to DDname SYSEXEC or SYSPROC during your TSO session, you can execute it by entering the following on the command line of any ISPF panel:

```
TSO %SCANSEQ
     or
TSO %SCANSEQ dsn
```

Note: dsn must be replaced by the fully or partially qualified name of the dataset you wish to scan.

Let us see how this exec works. On line 10 it obtains the fully qualified or the partial name of the sequential dataset. Then on line 11 it checks if the user omitted dataset name from the command. If so, on lines 13–16 it prompts the user for the dataset name. If the user again enters a null string, the EXIT instruction on line 20 terminates the exec.

Suppose the dataset name entered is not null. On line 25 it checks if the dataset name is enclosed within single quotation marks. If not, the code on lines 27–31 adds the user's prefix at the beginning and inserts single quotation marks at the beginning and end of the dataset name. On lines 41–45 it prompts you to enter the string that is to be searched. If you entered a null value for the string, that is, if you just pressed the Enter key without entering anything, the exec will reject it and prompt you to reenter. On line 46 it allocates the dataset to DDname MYFILE. On line 48 it checks if the return code from the ALLOCATE command is nonzero. If so, this indicates that the allocation failed, in which case the exec displays a number of lines of messages on lines 50–53 and then executes the EXIT instruction on line 54 to terminate the exec.

If the ALLOC command was successful, control flows to line 57 where FINITO is initialized to NO. On line 60 the DO WHILE loop is started whose END is on line 76. In this loop, on line 61

```
****************************************************************************
1  /****************** REXX ******************************************/
2  /* THIS EXEC SHOWS HOW TO READ AN ENTIRE SEQUENTIAL DATASET, ONE  */
3  /* RECORD AT A TIME. EACH RECORD IS EXAMINED FOR THE PRESENCE OF A */
4  /* GIVEN STRING. IF FOUND, THE RECORD NUMBER AND THE RECORD ARE    */
5  /* DISPLAYED ON THE TERMINAL. THE RECORD LENGTH OF THE SEQUENTIAL FILE*/
6  /* CAN BE ANYTHING.                                               */
7  /* AUTHOR: BARRY K. NIRMAL                                        */
8  /****************************************************************/
9  TRACE ALL
10 ARG DSN .
11 IF DSN = '' THEN
12   DO
13     SAY 'THE DATASET NAME  PASSED TO THIS EXEC IS NULL'
14     SAY 'PLEASE ENTER THE NAME OF THE SEQUENTIAL DATASET'
15     SAY '(ENTERING A NULL VALUE WILL TERMINATE THIS EXEC.)'
16     PULL DSN
17     IF DSN = '' THEN
18       DO
19         SAY 'THIS EXEC IS NOW TERMINATING'
20         EXIT
21       END
22     ELSE NOP
23   END
24 ELSE NOP
25 IF SUBSTR(DSN,1,1) \= '7D'X THEN
26   DO
27     DSN = INSERT('.',DSN,0)
28     PREF = SYSVAR(SYSPREF)
```

```
29  DSN = INSERT(PREF,DSN,0)
30  DSN = INSERT('7D'X,DSN,0)
31  DSN = INSERT('7D'X,DSN,LENGTH(DSN))
32  END
33  ELSE NOP
34  /******************************************************************/
35  /* AT THIS POINT, DSN CONTAINS FULLY-QUALIFIED DATASET NAME ENCLOSED  */
36  /* WITHIN SINGLE QUOTATION MARKS.                                     */
37  /******************************************************************/
38  SAY 'THIS EXEC WILL SCAN THE FOLLOWING SEQUENTIAL DATASET FOR THE '
39  SAY 'PRESENCE OF A STRING:'
40  SAY '   ' DSN
41  STRING = ''
42  DO WHILE STRING = ''
43      SAY 'KINDLY ENTER THE STRING TO BE SEARCHED'
44      PULL STRING
45  END
46  "ALLOC F(MYFILE) DA("DSN"") SHR REUSE "
47  RETCODE = RC
48  IF RETCODE \= 0 THEN
49      DO
50          SAY 'AN ERROR OCCURRED IN ALLOCATING THE SEQUENTIAL DATASET'
51          SAY 'THE RETURN CODE FROM THE ALLOC COMMAND WAS:' RETCODE
52          SAY 'PLEASE INVESTIGATE THIS PROBLEM, CORRECT THE ERROR AND RETRY'
53          SAY 'THIS EXEC MET WITH AN ACCIDENT AND DIED IN A HURRY'
54          EXIT
55      END
56  ELSE NOP
57  FINITO = 'NO'
```

Figure 2.16. An exec to scan all records of a sequential file for a specified string. *continues*

59

```
58    RECNUM = 0
59    MATCH_COUNT = 0
60    DO WHILE FINITO = 'NO'
61      "EXECIO 1 DISKR MYFILE "
62      IF RC = 0 THEN
63        DO
64          PULL RECORD
65          RECNUM = RECNUM + 1
66          IF INDEX(RECORD,STRING) \= 0 THEN
67            DO
68              MATCH_COUNT = MATCH_COUNT + 1
69              SAY 'YOUR STRING WAS FOUND IN RECORD NUMBER' RECNUM,
70                  'WHICH IS AS FOLLOWS'
71              SAY RECORD
72            END
73          ELSE NOP
74        END
75      ELSE FINITO = 'YES'
76    END
77    SAY 'TOTAL RECORDS READ FROM THE SEQUENTIAL FILE:' RECNUM
78    IF MATCH_COUNT = 0 THEN
79      SAY 'YOUR STRING WAS NOT FOUND IN THE SEQUENTIAL DATASET'
80    ELSE
81      SAY 'YOUR STRING WAS FOUND IN' MATCH_COUNT 'RECORD(S)'
82    "EXECIO 0 DISKR MYFILE (FINIS "      /* CLOSE THE FILE */
83    "FREE F(MYFILE) "                    /*FREE THE FILE   */
84    EXIT
*******************************************************************************
```

Figure 2.16. (Continued)

the EXECIO command reads the next record from the dataset allocated to DDname MYFILE. If end-of-file occurred, the value of RC would be nonzero. So, on line 62 we check if RC is zero. If so, the DO loop started on line 63 would be entered. This DO loop has its END on line 74.

Suppose that a record was successfully read. On line 64 we pull that record from the top of the stack and put it in variable RECORD. On line 66 the INDEX built-in function is used to check if RECORD contains the string contained in STRING. If so, lines 68–71 would be executed. On these lines we display the record number and the record itself.

Eventually, the EXECIO command would encounter end-of-file. This would send control to line 75 where FINITO would be set to YES. Next, the END on line 76 would send control to the DO WHILE on 60. Since FINITO is no longer NO, an exit would be taken from the DO WHILE loop. Control would then flow to line 77 where a message would be displayed. Finally, the EXIT instruction on line 84 would terminate the exec, sending control to TSO/ISPF.

2.15. AN EXEC TO WRITE A SINGLE RECORD OF ALL 9s IN ANY SEQUENTIAL DATASET

Suppose you have defined a key-sequenced VSAM file whose record length is 300. You want to initialize this file by writing into it a 300-bytes-long record, containing 9 in all positions. How do you do this? Follow these steps:

- Allocate a sequential file with logical record length of 300. You can do this using option 3.2 (Utility-Dataset) of ISPF.
- Write into this sequential file a record that has 9 in all positions.
- Using IDCAMS REPRO, copy the content of the sequential file into your VSAM file.

"But how do I write a record of 300 bytes into my sequential file?" you might ask. You can't do it using ISPF Editor, because ISPF can't be used to edit a dataset that has record length of 256 or more. So how do you do it?

"Write a COBOL program that will do this," you might reply. But why not write a REXX exec? It's so much easier. In Figure 2.17

```
1  /*****************************  REXX  **************************************/
2  /* Author: Barry K. Nirmal                                               */
3  /***********************************************************************/
4  /* This EXEC will write a single record of 300 bytes into a sequential*/
5  /* file that has record length of 300. The record written will contain*/
6  /* 9 in all positions.                                                 */
7  /***********************************************************************/
8  /* This EXEC can be easily modified to write into a file that has      */
9  /* record length other than 300. See lines with 'Check' in comments.   */
10 /* This EXEC can also be easily modified to write multiple records     */
11 /* into a file, thus facilitating creation of test files for testing   */
12 /* programs.                                                           */
13 /***********************************************************************/
14 /* If record length of file is less than 300, RC will be nonzero when  */
15 /* EXECIO is executed, but a record with 9 in all positions will get   */
16 /* successfully written into the file.                                 */
17 /***********************************************************************/
18 /* If record length of file is greater than 300, RC will be zero when  */
19 /* EXECIO is executed; a record will get written, but only the first   */
```

```
20  /* 300 bytes of the record will contain 9 in all positions.        */
21  /*****************************************************************/
22  Barry = ""
23  "Allocate f(bknfile) da(junk300) shr"    /* Check LRECL of data set */
24  do i = 0 to 299                          /* Check the upper limit used */
25     Barry = Insert('9',Barry,I)
26  End
27  Push Barry
28  "execio 1 diskw bknfile (FINIS"
29  If RC ¬= 0 then
30     Say 'Sir/Madam: Error occurred when writing record to file'
31  Else
32     Do
33        Say "Sir/Madam: A single record consisting of all 9's has been"
34        Say "successfully written into the sequential file."
35     End
36  "Free f(bknfile)"
37  EXIT 0
*****************************************************************
```

Figure 2.17.   An exec to write a single record into a dataset.

is an exec that will do this job. If you don't take into account the comments, you will find that this is a very short exec. Writing it is much simpler than writing a COBOL program, or even an SAS or Easytrieve program. Read the comments in this figure. They explain how this exec works and the various issues involved such as what happens if this exec is used with a dataset that has record length less than or greater than 300. Note that if the record length of the file is greater than 300, the record written will contain 9 in the first 300 positions and blanks in the remaining positions.

Explanation of this exec. When you issue the command to invoke this exec, execution starts from line 22 in Figure 2.17, which is the first noncomment line. Here variable BARRY is being initialized to null, that is, nothing. On the next line we allocate dataset 'prefix.JUNK300' to DDname BKNFILE, where prefix is the user's TSO prefix. Supposedly this dataset has record length of 300. (See the comments on lines 14 –20 to know what would happen if it is not.) On the next line we start a DO loop with variable I taking successive values from 0 to 299. On line 25 we insert character 9 in variable BARRY after leaving I characters from the beginning. This is what will happen:

Value of I	Value of BARRY after line 25 has executed
0	9
1	99
2	999
3	9999
299	A string containing 300 occurrences of 9

When control reaches line 27, BARRY will contain a string containing 300 occurrences of 9. On line 27 variable BARRY is written to the top of the stack. On line 28 the item on the top of the stack is written to file BKNFILE, and then the file is closed. (It is the presence of (FINIS that closes the file.) If the EXECIO command was successful, RC would be zero. On line 29 we check if RC is nonzero, that is, if the EXECIO failed. If so, the Say instruction on line 30 would be executed; otherwise lines 33 and 34 would be executed. Finally, on line 36 the DDname BKNFILE is freed up. The EXIT instruction on line 37 terminates this exec and control flows to TSO, because it was TSO that had transferred control to this exec.

2.16. AN EXEC FOR COPYING AN ENTIRE DATASET INTO ANOTHER

How do you copy an entire sequential file into another? "Using IEBGENER" is the reply most likely to be heard, because IEBGENER is one of the oldest and most frequently used utilities in the MVS world. But why not use the new commands available with TSO/E Version 2 and REXX? Figure 2.18 shows a REXX exec that copies all records from one sequential file to another. The main purpose of this exec is not only to show you the technique of copying an entire sequential file into another, but also to illustrate the use of EXECIO, NEWSTACK, and DELSTACK commands. Take a few minutes to study this exec.

Suppose you have a dataset named 'prefix.W1' where prefix stands for your TSO prefix. It is the input dataset. Dataset 'prefix.W2' may or may not exist. It is the output dataset. You want to copy all records from the input file into the output file. If this facility has been installed as shown below, you can issue this command from the command line of any ISPF panel:

```
TSO %LOADSEQ W1 W2
```

If the output dataset exists, its contents will get overwritten with records in the input file. If the output dataset does not exist, it will be first allocated like the input file, prior to copying the input file into it.

Procedure for installing this exec

1. Copy the exec of Figure 3.12 (see Chapter 3) in member CHECKDSN of a PDS that is allocated to DDname SYSEXEC or SYSPROC during your TSO session.
2. Copy the exec of Figure 2.18 into member LOADSEQ of the same PDS in which you copied CHECKDSN.

```rexx
1   /*********************** REXX ***********************/
2   /* AUTHOR: BARRY KUMAR NIRMAL                       */
3   /*************************************************** /
4   ARG OLD_DSN NEW_DSN
5   CHECKDSN OLD_DSN
6   IF RC ¬= 0 THEN
7    DO
8      SAY 'THE INPUT FILE IS NOT CATALOGED OR NOT AVAILABLE'
9      SAY 'SO, I AM TERMINATING QUICKLY'
10     EXIT
11   END
12  CHECKDSN NEW_DSN
13  IF RC = 2 THEN
14   DO
15     SAY 'THE OUTPUT FILE IS NOT CATALOGED'
16     SAY 'SO, I WILL TRY TO ALLOCATE IT LIKE THE INPUT FILE'
17     "ALLOC F(OUTFILE) DA("NEW_DSN") LIKE("OLD_DSN") NEW"
18     IF RC ¬= 0 THEN
19      DO
20       SAY 'I COULD NOT ALLOCATE THE OUTPUT FILE'
21       SAY 'SO, I AM QUICKLY TERMINATIONG MYSELF. GOODBYE'
```

```
22              EXIT
23           END
24        END
25     ELSE IF RC = 0 THEN
26        "ALLOC F(OUTFILE) DA("NEW_DSN"") SHR REUSE"
27     ELSE
28        DO
29           SAY 'THE OUTPUT FILE IS IN USE BY SOMEONE ELSE'
30           SAY 'SO I AM TERMINATING QUICKLY'
31           EXIT
32        END
33     "ALLOC F(INFILE) DA("OLD_DSN"") SHR REUSE"
34     "NEWSTACK"
35     "EXECIO * DISKR INFILE (FINIS"
36     NUMREC = QUEUED()
37     "EXECIO" NUMREC "DISKW OUTFILE (FINIS "
38     "DELSTACK "
39     "FREE F(INFILE OUTFILE) "
40     SAY 'SIR/MADAM, COPYING OF INPUT FILE INTO OUTPUT FILE IS DONE'
41     EXIT
********************************************************************************
```

Figure 2.18.   An exec to copy any sequential file into another.

Explanation of this exec. Let us see what the exec of Figure 2.18 does. On line 5 we issue command CHECKDSN, passing it the name of the input dataset. This will invoke the exec of Figure 3.12. CHECKDSN will return 0 if the input file exists; otherwise it will return a nonzero return code. On line 6 we check the return code set by CHECKDSN. If it is nonzero, lines 8, 9, and 10 would be executed, and this exec would terminate; otherwise control would flow to line 12. Here we issue the CHECKDSN command, passing it the name of the output file. If the output file does not exist, on line 17 we would allocate it with the same characteristics as the input dataset. (Using the LIKE operand means that we don't have to enter operands such as dataset organization, logical record length, record format, space required in tracks, etc. on the ALLOC command.) If the output file exists, it would get allocated on line 26.

On line 33 we allocate the input file under DDname INFILE. The REUSE option lets us allocate this DDname, even if it is already allocated, without first having to free it. The SHR option lets multiple users use this dataset concurrently. This allocation will work because we have already verified that this dataset exists.

On line 34 the NEWSTACK command is used to create a new stack to isolate data on the old stack. Whenever we copy a number of lines to and from the data stack, it is a good idea to use the NEWSTACK and DELSTACK commands. This prevents the exec from inadvertently removing items that may already be present on the stack. For more information about these commands, read "Protecting Elements in the Data Stack" in Chapter 11 of IBM's *TSO Extensions Version 2 REXX User's Guide.*

On line 35 all records are read from the dataset allocated to DDname INFILE and placed on the new data stack created using NEWSTACK. The (FINIS option means that INFILE will be closed after the read operation. This is necessary so that we can later free up this DDname. On line 36 we use the QUEUED built-in function to determine the number of records present on the data stack and store that number in variable NUMREC. On line 37 we are specifying that NUMREC number of records should be written from the data stack to the file allocated to DDname OUTFILE. This results in the writing of all the records from the stack. The (FINIS option specifies that OUTFILE should be closed at the end of the write operation. This is needed so that later we can free up DDname. On line 38 we delete the data stack created earlier. On line 39 the two DDnames allocated earlier are freed up. The EXIT instruction on line 41 terminates this exec.

2.17. AN EXEC FOR UPDATING A SINGLE LINE IN A DATASET

In Section 2.8 we discussed a REXX exec that changes one line in a dataset and then submits the job in it. That exec is shown in Figure 2.10, and the job is shown in Figure 2.9. Let us now write another exec called JOBSUB that can replace the exec shown in Figure 2.10. The user will invoke this exec by entering the following:

```
TSO %JOBSUB ssss
```

where ssss will be replaced by a suitable four-character string by the user. This exec will read the dataset shown in Figure 2.9. The first line in this dataset is supposed to contain a valid JOB statement. It will change line 7, which has the EXEC statement, to the following:

```
//STEP01 EXEC CICSssss
```

where ssss will be replaced by the actual string supplied by the user. Such a REXX exec is shown in Figure 2.19.

Explanation of this exec. Suppose the user enters the following to invoke this exec:

```
TSO JOBSUB PRD2
```

After line 2 has executed, USERDATA will contain string PRD2. On line 3 variable LEN is assigned the value 4, because the length of the string contained in USERDATA is 4. On line 4 we are assigning a value to NEWLINE. On line 5 we are inserting the string contained in USERDATA in the string contained in NEWLINE after leaving 18 positions from the beginning. (Read the description of the INSERT built-in function in IBM's *TSO/E*

```
01   /****************** REXX *********************
02   ARG USERDATA
03   LEN = LENGTH(USERDATA)
04   NEWLINE = '//STEP01 EXEC CICS'
05   NEWLINE = INSERT(USERDATA,NEWLINE,18,LEN)
06   "ALLOC F(MYFILE) DA(JOBS.CNTL(PROCSCAN)) SHR"
07   "EXECIO 1 DISKRU MYFILE 7 (LIFO"
08   PULL RECORD
09   SAY 'RECORD 7 READ FROM FILE IS: ' RECORD
10   PUSH NEWLINE
11   "EXECIO 1 DISKW MYFILE (FINIS "
12   SAY 'RECORD 7 REWRITTEN TO THE FILE IS ' NEWLINE
13   "SUBMIT JOBS.CNTL(PROCSCAN)"
14   "FREE F(MYFILE) "
15   EXIT
```

Figure 2.19.   An exec showing how to update a specific line in a dataset and submit the job in it.

Version 2 REXX Reference to find more about it.) On line 6 member PROCSCAN of PDS 'prefix.JOBS.CNTL' is allocated to DDname MYFILE with the disposition of SHR. (At the execution time, prefix will be replaced by the TSO prefix of the user executing this exec.) On line 7 we use the EXECIO command to read record number 7 from the dataset allocated to MYFILE. (In this command, 1 specifies that we want to read one record, and 7 specifies that we want to read record number 7. The LIFO option is specifying that the record should go on the stack in LIFO order, i.e., Last In First Out. This will place the record on the top of the stack. The default order is FIFO, i.e., First In First Out. This places the record at the bottom of the stack.) To get sound concepts of the data stack mechanism used in REXX, read "Storing Information in the Data Stack" in Chapter 11 of IBM's *TSO/E Version 2 REXX User's Guide.*

On line 8 we pull off the record read from the top of the stack. (Note: In REXX an item can be placed on the top or at the bottom of the stack, but it is removed from the top of the stack only.) On line 10 we place the content of NEWLINE on the top of the stack.

On line 11 the item placed on the stack top by the PUSH instruction is removed from the stack and rewritten to the file allocated to DDname MYFILE, and then the file is closed. (In this command, 1 specifies that we want to write just one record from the stack. FINIS specifies that the file should be closed after the write operation has completed.) On line 13 the content of dataset 'prefix.JOBS.CNTL(PROCSCAN)' is submitted as a batch job. On the next line, DDname MYFILE is freed up. The EXIT instruction on line 15 terminates this exec and control flows to TSO.

Notes on this exec

1. Why did we read the seventh record on line 7? Because this is how things must be done. You must use the DISKRU form of the EXECIO command to read the record that you want to subsequently update.

2. This exec shows that when we want to update a single line in a dataset, it is more efficient to first find out the line number we want to update and specify it on the read operation, rather than read all the lines in the dataset to the stack, locate and change the line, and then write out all the records.

3. Suppose we comment out line 7 in this exec. When the PULL instruction on line 8 is executed, since there is nothing on the stack, information from the terminal will be pulled. This means that the exec will wait until the user enters something on the terminal. This means that the PULL and the PARSE PULL instructions are used not only to extract information from the terminal, but also to remove information from the data stack.

3

Some More Useful REXX Execs for Everyone

3.1.   AN EXEC TO PROCESS A ONE-DIMENSIONAL ARRAY

An array is essentially an organized collection of data. An array can be one-dimensional, two-dimensional, and so on up to n-dimensional, where n can be an infinite number. For most business applications, though, a three-dimensional array is the most one deals with. Suppose the Finance Department of our company has 25 employees. We want to write an exec that will store the last name and monthly salary of each employee in the form of arrays. We will use one one-dimensional array to store the last names of employees, and another one-dimensional array to store their monthly salaries. Thus the collection of 25 monthly salaries can be considered a one-dimensional array or a vector. In mathematical language, Vector A of size n is represented by its n components:

$$a_1 \quad a_2 \quad a_3 \quad \ldots \quad a_n$$

Figure 3.1 shows the value of each element of this array, where the value of each element represents an employee's monthly salary.

The problem. Let us write a REXX exec that will prompt the user for the number of employees. (This is to make the exec flex-

```
*****************************************************************
                                Value of Array Element
          Array Element        (Monthly Salary in U.S.
          Number               Dollars)

              1                         2500
              2                         4110
              3                         5100
          -  -  -  -  -  -  -  -  -  -  -  -  -  -  -
          -  -  -  -  -  -  -  -  -  -  -  -  -  -
             25                         3500
*****************************************************************
```

Figure 3.1.   A one-dimensional array with 25 elements.

ible, so that we need not change it every time an employee leaves or joins the department and the employee count changes. This flexibility is an important feature of well-designed programs.) It will then prompt the user for the last name of employee 1, and then his or her monthly salary. Next it will prompt the user for the last name of employee 2 and monthly salary. This will be continued for employee 3, 4, . . . n where n is the employee count initially entered by the user.

This exec will store the last names of all the employees in one one-dimensional array. It will store the monthly salaries of all the employees in another one-dimensional array. At the end it will display in a tabular fashion the following fields: employee number, last name, and monthly salary. One example of the man–machine dialog is shown in Figure 3.2. Note: In this figure SYS stands for system prompt or response to operator command, and OPR stands for operator command or response to system prompt.

The solution. The exec that will solve this problem is shown in Figure 3.3. Let us discuss how it works. If this exec is stored in member ARRAY1 in a PDS that is allocated to DDname SYSEXEC

```
************************************************************
SYS: ENTER THE NUMBER OF EMPLOYEES IN THE FINANCE DEPT
     The value entered must be between 1 and 100
OPR: 25
SYS: Enter the last name of employee number 1 please
     (Only the first 30 characters of data entered will be used)
OPR: smith
SYS: Enter the monthly salary of employee number 1
OPR: 2500
SYS: Enter the last name of employee number 2 please
     (Only the first 30 characters of data entered will be used)
OPR: jones
SYS: Enter the monthly salary of employee number 2
OPR: 4110
     - - - - -
     - - - - -
SYS:
     Employee      Last Name               Monthly Salary
     Number                                 in US Dollars
     **********    *******************************    ****************
     1             SMITH                   2500
     2             JONES                   4110
     - - - - -
     - - - - -

************************************************************
```

Figure 3.2.   One example of man–machine dialogue when the exec of Figure 3.3 is executed.

75

```
***********************************************************************
 1  /****************** REXX ***********************************/
 2  /* This exec will prompt you for a count of employees in the finance */
 3  /* dept. It will then prompt you for the last name and monthly salary */
 4  /* of each employee. It will store the data entered in two one- */
 5  /* dimensional arrays. At the end, it will display the data entered */
 6  /* for all employees. The display will be in the form of a table. */
 7  /****************************************************************/
 8  Toprompt = 'yes'
 9  Do while toprompt = 'yes'
10    SAY 'ENTER THE NUMBER OF EMPLOYEES IN THE FINANCE DEPT'
11    SAY 'The value entered must be between 1 and 100'
12    Pull Maxele
13    If Datatype(maxele) ¬= 'NUM' Then
14      Say 'The value entered for employee count is not numeric'
15    Else
16      If maxele ¬> 0 | maxele > 100  Then
17        Say 'The value of employee count entered is not between 1 and 100'
18      Else toprompt = 'no'
19  END
20  Do element = 1 to maxele
21    data = ' '
22    Do while data = ' '
23      Say 'enter the last name of employee number ' element ' please'
24      Say '(Only the first 30 characters of data entered will be used)'
25      Pull data
26    End
```

76

```
27  lastname.element = ''
28  lastname.element = Insert(data,lastname.element,0,30)
29  toprompt = 'yes'
30  Do while toprompt = 'yes'
31    Say 'Enter the monthly salary of employee number ' element
32    Pull aa
33    If datatype(aa) ¬= 'NUM' Then
34      Say 'Salary entered for employee is not numeric'
35    Else
36      if aa -> 0 | aa > 99999.99  Then
37        Say 'Salary entered is not greater than 0 and less than 100000.00'
38      Else toprompt = 'no'
39    End
40    salary.element = aa
41  End
42  Say 'Employee   Last Name                        Monthly Salary'
43  Say 'Number                                      in US Dollars '
44  Say '*********  *************************************************** '
45  Do I = 1 to maxele
46    Number = ''
47    Number = insert(i,number,0,10)
48    Say Number   lastname.i    salary.I
49  end
50  Exit 0
```

`****************************************************************************`

Figure 3.3.   An exec to process one-dimensional arrays.

or SYSPROC during your TSO session, you can execute it by issuing this command on any ISPF panel:

```
TSO %ARRAY1
```

Execution will start from line 8 in Figure 3.3, which is the first noncomment line. On line 9 we start a DO WHILE loop whose END is on line 19. In this loop, we prompt the user for the number of employees. On line 12 the value entered on the terminal is captured and stored in variable MAXELE. On line 13 we are checking if the data entered is numeric. If not, line 14 will get executed, or else control will flow to line 16. On line 16 we check if the data entered is between 1 to 100, inclusive. If not, the SAY instruction on line 17 will get executed. If the value entered is between 1 and 100, line 18 will get executed where TOPROMPT will be set to NO. Let us suppose that the user entered 25 for the number of employees.

Setting TOPROMPT to NO on line 18 means that when the END on line 19 is executed and control will flow to line 9, since TOPROMPT is not YES, we will exit the DO WHILE loop and control will flow to line 20. Here we start a DO loop whose END is on line 41. This DO loop will be executed with control variable ELEMENT taking successive values from 1 to MAXELE.

Let us see what happens in this DO loop. Suppose this is the first time through the loop and the value of control variable ELEMENT is 1. On lines 22–26, we prompt the user for the last name of the employee. If the user did not enter anything, that is, if he simply pressed the Enter key, the DO loop on lines 22–26 would get executed again. This is a good technique of ensuring that the user must enter something when prompted for data. When control reaches line 27, variable DATA contains what the user entered. On line 28 we store the first 30 characters of DATA in variable LASTNAME.1. (If DATA contains a string shorter than 30 characters, there is no problem. The remaining positions in LASTNAME.1 will be padded with blanks.)

On line 30 we start a DO WHILE loop whose END is on line 39. In this loop, we will prompt the user for the monthly salary of this first employee and store it in variable SALARY.1. As before, in this loop we verify that the data entered by the user is numeric and that it is greater than zero and less than one hundred thousand. (It is very unlikely that an employee's monthly salary is either zero or one hundred thousand dollars or more.) If it is not, the user will be prompted again for the value of salary.

Now ELEMENT will assume the value of 2, and the DO loop enclosed within lines 20 and 41 will be executed again. This time, in this loop data will be stored in variables LASTNAME.2 and SALARY.2. This process will be repeated with ELEMENT assuming successive values from 3 to MAXELE. Finally, compound variables LASTNAME.1, LASTNAME.2, LASTNAME.3, . . . , LASTNAME.25, and SALARY.1, SALARY.2, . . . , SALARY.25 will contain valid values. (These are called compound variables because there is at least one period in their names with characters on both sides of it.) On lines 42–44 we display the headings. On lines 45–49 we execute a DO loop in which the values for number, last name, and salary for each employee are displayed on the terminal. Finally, when line 50 executes, this REXX exec terminates and control flows to TSO.

This exec shows illustrates the following techniques:

- How to use the TOPROMPT switch to keep on prompting the user until he or she has entered valid data.
- How to store data in one-dimensional arrays using compound variables.
- How to display data in columns.
- Even if data entered on the terminal is of varying length, how to store it in a variable of fixed length, so that it can be displayed properly in a tabular fashion. For example, in this exec the length of LASTNAME.1, LASTNAME.2, and so on will always be 30, even though the length of variable DATA entered on the terminal will vary. If the user entered BUSH, the length of DATA will be 4; if he entered NIRMAL, it will be 6.

3.2. AN EXEC TO PROCESS A TWO-DIMENSIONAL ARRAY

A two-dimensional array is essentially a table of information. In mathematical language, it is called a matrix. The elements of a k by l matrix are represented by the subscript notation:

$$a_{11} \ldots a_{1j} \ldots a_{1l}$$
$$a_{21} \ldots a_{2j} \ldots a_{2l}$$
$$------------$$
$$------------$$
$$a_{k1} \ldots a_{kj} \ldots a_{kl}$$

For example, Figure 3.4 shows a 4 by 6 matrix. There are six columns in this matrix. The first column represents the number of courses completed by an employee in the year 1989. The second column represents the number of courses completed in the year 1990, and so on. Finally, the sixth column represents the total number of courses completed by an employee in the years 1989 through 1993. The first row represents the first employee, named Hollinger. The second row stands for the second employee, named Tiwary, and so on. Finally, the fourth row represents the fourth employee, named Hudders. Normally all elements of a matrix are of the same data type. This makes it easy to load the entire matrix into storage by a high-level language such as COBOL or REXX. All elements of the matrix in Figure 3.4 are whole numbers.

The problem. The problem is to write a REXX exec that will prompt the user for the total number of employees in the department. It will then prompt the user for the last name of each employee. All the last names will be stored in a one-dimensional

```
**************************************************************
               Number of Courses Completed in the Year
Employee's     1989    1990    1991    1992    1993   TOTAL
Last Name

HOLLINGER       2       2       0       1       2       7
TIWARY          0       1       2       0       3       6
SMITH           1       1       2       1       1       6
HUDDERS         1       0       2       2       1       6
**************************************************************
```

Figure 3.4.   A two-dimensional array with 4 rows and 6 columns (a 4 by 6 matrix).

array. Next it will pick the first employee, and prompt the user to enter the number of courses completed by him or her in the years 1989 through 1993. It will then pick the second employee and prompt the user to enter the number of courses completed during the same years. This will be repeated for employee numbers 3, 4, 5, and so on up to the last employee. Finally, the exec will compute the total number of courses completed by each employee and display them. One example of the man–machine dialog is shown in Figure 3.5. Note: In this figure SYS stands for system prompt or response to operator command, and OPR stands for operator command or response to system prompt.

The solution. One REXX exec that solves this problem is shown in Figure 3.6. Let us see how it works. If this exec is stored in member EMPARRAY of a PDS that is allocated to DDname SYSEXEC or SYSPROC during your TSO session, you can execute it by issuing this command on any ISPF panel:

```
TSO %EMPARRAY
```

Execution will start from line 6 in Figure 3.6, which is the first noncomment line. On line 7 we start a DO WHILE loop whose END is on line 17. In this loop we prompt the user for the employee count. On line 10 the data entered by the user is stored in variable TOTEMP. On line 11 we check if the value of TOTEMP is not numeric. If so, line 12 would be executed, or else line 14 would get control. On line 14 we check if the employee count entered by the user is in the range 1 to 100, inclusive. If not, line 15 would be executed. If the value of TOTEMP is in the range 1 to 100, line 16 would be executed.

Suppose the user entered 25 for employee count. In this case, on line 16 TOPROMPT would be set to NO. As a result, when line 17 is executed and control flows to line 7, an exit would be taken from the DO WHILE loop because TOPROMPT is not YES. Control would flow to line 18.

On line 18 we start a DO loop whose END is on line 28. In this loop, we prompt the user for the last name of each employee, starting from the first employee and going up to the last employee. For the first employee, the last name is stored in variable

```
************************************************************

SYS: Enter the total number of employees in the department:
     (The value entered must be between 1 and 100.)
OPR: 25
SYS: Enter the last name of employee number 1 please
     (Only the first 30 characters of data entered will be used)
OPR: hollinger
SYS: Enter the last name of employee number 2 please
     (Only the first 30 characters of data entered will be used)
OPR: tiwary
- - - - -
- - - - -

SYS: Enter the number of courses successfully completed by: HOLLINGER
     For The Year 1989
OPR: 2
SYS:  For The year 1990
OPR: 2
SYS:  For The year 1991
OPR: 0
SYS:  For The year 1992
OPR: 1
SYS:  For The year 1993
OPR: 2
```

```
SYS: Enter the number of courses successfully completed by: TIWARY
        For The Year 1989

OPR: 0
SYS:    For The year 1990
OPR: 1
SYS:    For The year 1991
OPR: 2
SYS:    For The year 1992
OPR: 0
SYS:    For The year 1993
OPR: 3
     - - - -
     - - - -
SYS:
     Total number of courses completed by HOLLINGER = 7
     Total number of courses completed by TIWARY = 6
     - - -
     - - -
**************************************************************
```

Figure 3.5.   One example of man–machine dialogue when the exec of Figure 3.6 is executed.

83

```rexx
     /*****************************************************************/
 1   /*************** REXX ************************************/
 2   /* Exec name: EMPARRAY      Author: Barry K. Nirmal      */
 3   /* Shows how to store data in two-dimensional arrays. Also shows how */
 4   /* to process data stored in two-dimensional arrays.    */
 5   /*****************************************************************/
 6   Toprompt = 'yes'
 7   Do while toprompt = 'yes'
 8     SAY 'Enter the total number of employees in the department:'
 9     SAY '(The value entered must be between 1 and 100.)'
10     Pull totemp
11     If Datatype(totemp) ¬= 'NUM' Then
12        Say 'The value entered for employee count is not numeric'
13     Else
14        If totemp ¬> 0 | totemp > 100  Then
15           Say 'The value of employee count entered is not between 1 and 100'
16        Else toprompt = 'no'
17   END
18   Do item = 1 to totemp
19     data = ''
20     Do while data = ''
21        Say 'Enter the last name of employee number ' item ' please'
22        Say '(Only the first 30 characters of data entered will be used)'
23        Pull data
24     End
25     lastname.item = data
26     Barry = ''
27     lastname30.item = Insert(data,Barry,0,30)
28   End
```

```
29  Do I = 1 to totemp
30    Say 'Enter the number of courses successfully completed by: ',
31        lastname.I
32    Message3 = '    For the year 1989 '
33    datamax = 99
34    Call getnumdata
35    count.i.1989 = data
36    Do j = 1990 to 1993
37      message3 = '    For the Year   ' j
38      CALL getnumdata
39      count.i.j = data
40    End
41  End
/****************************************************************/
/* Now for each employee, calculate the total number of courses  */
/* completed for the five years (1989 - 1993) and store the total in */
/* the sixth column of the array. The first five columns of the array */
/* represent the total number of courses completed by an employee in */
/* the years 1989, 1990, 1991, 1992 and 1993.                        */
/****************************************************************/
49  Do i = 1 to totemp
50    tot = 0
51    Do j = 1989 to 1993
52      tot = tot + count.i.j
53    End
54    count.i.$$$ = tot
55    Say 'Total number of courses completed by ' lastname.i ' ' = ' count.i.$$$
56  End
57  Exit 0
```

Figure 3.6.   An exec to process two-dimensional arrays.

continues

```
58  /****************************************************************/
59  /* The following is an internal subroutine.                  */
60  /****************************************************************/
61  getnumdata:
62  Toprompt = 'yes'
63  Do while toprompt = 'yes'
64  SAY message3
65  Pull data
66  If Datatype(data) ¬= 'NUM' Then
67      Say 'The data you entered is not numeric'
68  Else
69      If data < 0 | data > datamax Then
70          Do
71              Say 'The data you entered is less than zero or greater than '
72              Say datamax ', which is the maximum allowed.'
73          End
74      Else toprompt = 'no'
75  END
76  Return
****************************************************************************************
```

Figure 3.6. (Continued)

LASTNAME.1; for the second employee, in LASTNAME.2; and so on. This way all the elements of this one-dimensional array would be assigned valid values.

On line 29 we start a DO loop whose END is on line 41. This loop would be executed for each employee. Let us suppose that this is the first time through the loop, that is, control variable I is 1. Say the last name of the first employee is HOLLINGER. On line 30, we would display this:

```
Enter the number of courses successfully completed
by: HOLLINGER
```

On line 33 we set DATAMAX to 99. (This is to tell GETNUMDATA that the number of courses entered by the user can't exceed 99.) On line 34 we call GETNUMDATA, which is an internal subroutine. Control flows to line 61. On line 63 a DO WHILE loop is started whose END is on line 75. On line 64 we display the content of variable MESSAGE3. (This variable was set on line 32.) The following prompt will appear on the screen:

```
For the year 1989
```

When the PULL instruction on line 65 is executed, this gives the user a chance the enter the data. Suppose he enters 2. On line 65 variable DATA would be assigned value 2. On line 66 we would check if the content of DATA is not numeric. In this example, this would be false, so control would flow to line 69. Here we would check if DATA is less than zero or greater than 99. (Remember, DATAMAX was set at 99 on line 33.) In this example, this would be true. Control would thus flow to line 74, then to line 75, and then to line 63. Since TOPROMPT is now NO, control would flow to line 76, where the RETURN instruction would send control back to line 35, because this line follows the line where this internal subroutine was invoked. On line 35 compound variable COUNT.1.1989 would be assigned the value contained in DATA, 2 in this example.

The DO loop started on line 36 has its END on line 40. In this loop the user would be prompted to enter the number of courses completed in the years 1990, 1991, 1992, and 1993. The values entered would be assigned to compound variables COUNT.1.1990,

COUNT.1.1991, COUNT.1.1992, and COUNT.1.1993. The END
on line 41 would send control to line 29, where I would be incremented
by 1. Control variable I now assumes the value of 2. The code on lines
30 through 40 would prompt the user to enter the number of courses
completed by the second employee for years 1989, 1990, 1991, 1992,
and 1993.

This way, the process described above would be repeated for
each employee up through the last employee. Finally, data for all
employees would be assigned in the following variables:

```
COUNT.1.1989 - Courses completed by employee 1 in 1989
COUNT.1.1990 - Courses completed by employee 1 in 1990
- - - -

- - - -

COUNT.2.1989 - Courses completed by employee 2 in 1989
COUNT.2.1990 - Courses completed by employee 2 in 1990
- - - -

- - - -

COUNT.25.1989 - Courses completed by employee 25 in 1989
COUNT.25.1990 - Courses completed by employee 25 in 1990
- - - -

- - - -

COUNT.25.1993 - Courses completed by employee 25 in 1993
```

On line 49 we start a DO loop whose END is in line 56. In this
loop we pick each employee and calculate the total number of
courses completed by him or her in years 1989 through 1993. The
total for the first employee is stored in variable COUNT.1.$$$,
for the second employee in variable COUNT.2.$$$, and so on. On
line 55 we display the total number of courses completed by the
particular employee being processed.

Finally, the DO WHILE loop started on line 49 would be exhausted, and control will flow to line 57. The EXIT instruction on
this line would terminate this exec and control would flow to TSO.

3.3. AN EXEC TO CALCULATE BLOCK SIZE AND SPACE REQUIREMENTS FOR ANY DATASET

The problem is to write a REXX exec that can be used to automate the task of calculating block sizes and space requirements

in tracks for datasets to be allocated by programmer/analysts. This exec, when invoked, will prompt the user for the following parameters:

- The logical record length of the dataset. (Dataset organization is assumed to be fixed blocked.)
- Initial choice of block size in terms of one-fifth track, one-sixth track, or one-seventh track blocking on an IBM 3380 DASD.
- The estimated number of logical records the dataset will contain.

This exec will then calculate and display the following parameters:

- The final block size value calculated based on the initial value for block size selected by the user.
- The primary track requirements for the dataset.
- The secondary track requirements for the dataset.
- The number of logical records to be contained in one track of IBM 3380 DASD based on the final block size value calculated.
- Percentage of track capacity utilized based on the block size calculated.

3.3.1.   How Can This EXEC Be Useful in Day-To-Day Work of Programmer/Analysts?

This REXX exec will be of immense help to the IS professionals who no longer have to look up a manual or a textbook to calculate the best values for the block sizes of their datasets. They can invoke this exec and obtain block sizes as well as space requirements that can be directly used in allocating the datasets either through TSO/ISPF (normally ISPF option 3.2) or through a batch job. Also the track capacity utilization calculated by this exec will indicate whether efficient use is being made of 3380 track capacity. To determine if this is the case, the user can invoke this exec again, entering some other value for the initial block size. The exec will then display another set of values for the parameters calculated. This way the programmer/analyst can compare the various values of block size and track utilization and select the best value for the block size.

It should be noted, however, that even if a lower value for block size results in a slightly better track utilization compared with a higher block size value, the higher value may be the best choice. This is due to the fact that a higher value for block size results in better utilization of CPU and channel. As I have said in my book:

> The optimization of the block sizes of sequential datasets is the most important factor in reducing CPU utilization. No other factor has anywhere near the potential for saving CPU cycles. It has been reported that in one experiment, increasing the block size of a sequential dataset from 200 bytes to 6K reduced CPU utilization by more than 87 percent and reduced channel time (EXCP) by 65 percent. (Nirmal, *Programming Standards and Guidelines, COBOL Edition,* Englewood Cliffs, NJ: Prentice-Hall, 1987, p. 203)

The solution. The REXX exec that solves this problem is shown in Figure 3.7. If this exec is stored in member HELPBLK of a PDS that is allocated to DDname SYSEXEC or SYSPROC during your TSO session, you can execute it by entering the following command on the command line of any ISPF panel:

```
TSO %HELPBLK
```

You are advised to study this exec thoroughly and be persuaded that it will faithfully and accurately calculate the various parameters as stated above.

Figure 3.8 displays some results returned by this exec based on the parameters supplied by the user.

Note: This exec can be easily modified to calculate best values for some other kind of DASD, such as IBM 3390.

```
   ****************************************************************
 1 /************** REXX ********************************************/
 2 /* THIS EXEC WILL ASK YOU TO ENTER THE RECORD LENGTH OF YOUR FIXED   */
 3 /* BLOCK FILE. IT WILL THEN ASK YOU WHETHER YOU WANT ONE-FIFTH, ONE- */
 4 /* SIXTH, OR ONE-SEVENTH TRACK BLOCKING ON IBM 3380 DASD. IT WILL THEN*/
 5 /* ASK YOU FOR THE ESTIMATED NUMBER OF RECORDS THIS FILE WILL CONTAIN.*/
 6 /* IT WILL THEN DO THE CALCULATIONS AND DISPLAY THE FOLLOWING PARA-   */
 7 /* METERS FOR USE IN ALLOCATING THE FILE THROUGH A BATCH JOB OR ISPF: */
 8 /*                                                                   */
 9 /*  - THE BLOCK SIZE                                                 */
10 /*  - THE PRIMARY NUMBER OF TRACKS REQUIRED                          */
11 /*  - THE SECONDARY NUMBER OF TRACKS REQUIRED                        */
12 /*  - THE NUMBER OF LOGICAL RECORDS CONTAINED IN ONE TRACK OF IBM 3380*/
13 /*    BASED ON YOUR CHOICE OF BLOCKING.                              */
14 /*******************************************************************/
15 /* IF THE USER DID NOT ENTER ANYTHING, I.E. IF HE SIMPLY PRESSED ENTER*/
16 /* KEY, THE VALUE OF VARIABLE OBTAINED BY USING THE PULL INSTRUCTION  */
17 /* WILL BE NULL. IT WILL NOT BE NUMERIC. SO, CHECKING THE VARIABLE IF */
18 /* IT IS NUMERIC IS SUFFICIENT TO ENSURE THAT THE USER ENTERED A      */
19 /* NUMBER.                                                           */
20 /* AUTHOR: BARRY K. NIRMAL                                           */
21 /*******************************************************************/
22 TOPROMPT = 'YES'
23 DO WHILE TOPROMPT = 'YES'
24   SAY 'ENTER LOGICAL RECORD LENGTH PLEASE'
25   PULL LRECL
```

Figure 3.7.   An exec to calculate optimum block size based on specified parameters. *continues*

```
26    IF DATATYPE(LRECL) = 'NUM' THEN
27      TOPROMPT = 'NO'
28    ELSE SAY 'THE LOGICAL RECORD LENGTH MUST BE NUMERIC'
29    END
30    TOPROMPT = 'YES'
31    DO WHILE TOPROMPT = 'YES'
32    SAY 'ENTER YOUR CHOICE OF BLOCKING FROM THE LIST BELOW:'
33    SAY ' '
34    SAY '5 = ONE FIFTH TRACK BLOCKING    (MAXIMUM BLOCKSIZE = 9,076)'
35    SAY '6 = ONE SIXTH TRACK BLOCKING    (MAXIMUM BLOCKSIZE = 7,476)'
36    SAY '7 = ONE SEVENTH TRACK BLOCKING  (MAXIMUM BLOCKSIZE = 6,356)'
37    SAY ' '
38    PULL FACTOR
39    IF FACTOR = 5 | FACTOR = 6 | FACTOR = 7 THEN
40      TOPROMPT = 'NO'
41    ELSE SAY 'ACCEPTABLE ANSWER IS 5, 6, OR 7 ONLY. YOUR ANSWER IS WRONG'
42    END
43    IF FACTOR = 5 THEN MAXBLKSIZE = 9076
44    IF FACTOR = 6 THEN MAXBLKSIZE = 7476
45    IF FACTOR = 7 THEN MAXBLKSIZE = 6356
46    IF LRECL > MAXBLKSIZE THEN
47    DO
48      SAY 'THE LOGICAL RECORD LENGTH YOU ENTERED IS GREATER THAN THE '
49      SAY 'MAXIMUM BLOCK SIZE BASED ON YOUR CHOICE OF BLOCKING'
50      SAY 'HENCE THIS EXEC IS ABNORMALLY TERMINATING... GOODBYE.....'
51      EXIT
52    END
53    TOPROMPT = 'YES'
54    DO WHILE TOPROMPT = 'YES'
55    SAY 'PLS ENTER THE ESTIMATED NUMBER OF RECORDS FOR THIS DATASET'
56    PULL NUMREC
57    IF DATATYPE(NUMREC) = 'NUM' THEN
```

```
59      ELSE SAY 'YOUR ANSWER IS NOT NUMERIC.'
60   END
61   BLKFACT = TRUNC(MAXBLKSIZE / LRECL)
62   BLKSIZE = BLKFACT * LRECL
63   TRACKS = TRUNC((NUMREC / BLKFACT) / FACTOR)
64   PRIMTRKS = TRACKS + 1
65   SECTRKS = TRUNC(PRIMTRKS / 10) + 1
66   RECPERTRK = BLKFACT * FACTOR
67   TRKUTIL = (RECPERTRK * LRECL * 100) / 47476
68   TRKUTIL = TRUNC(TRKUTIL,2)
69   SAY '                                                      '
70   SAY '   RECORD FORMAT            = FIXED BLOCK  '
71   SAY '   LOGICAL RECORD LENGTH    =' LRECL
72   SAY '   BLOCKSIZE                =' BLKSIZE
73   SAY '                                                      '
74   SAY '   PRIMARY  NUMBER OF TRACKS REQUIRED = ' PRIMTRKS
75   SAY '   SECONDARY NUMBER OF TRACKS REQUIRED = ' SECTRKS
76   SAY '                                                      '
77   SAY 'ONE TRACK WILL ACCOMODATE' RECPERTRK 'NUMBER OF LOGICAL RECORDS'
78   SAY 'TRACK CAPACITY UTILIZATION =' TRKUTIL ' PERCENT'
79   SAY '                                                      '
80   SAY 'IF YOU ARE CREATING THIS DATASET IN A BATCH JOB, PLEASE USE THE'
81   SAY 'FOLLOWING ALONG WITH DISP=(NEW,CATLG,DELETE):'
82   SAY '                                                      '
83   SAY '   DCB=(RECFM=FB,LRECL='LRECL',BLKSIZE='BLKSIZE'),'
84   SAY '   SPACE=(TRK,('PRIMTRKS','SECTRKS'),RLSE)'
85   SAY '                                                      '
86   SAY '                                                      '
87   EXIT
*************************************************************************
```

Figure 3.7. (Continued)

| <---- User Supplied ----> | | <------- Calculated by REXX Exec -----> | | | | |
Logical Record Length	Blocking Chosen by the User	Estimated Number of Records	Blocksize Calculated by Exec	Primary Number of Tracks	Secondary Number of Trks	Track Capacity Utilization
254	1/5th Track	2,000	8890	12	2	93.62 %
75	1/5th Track	4,000	9075	7	1	95.57 %
75	1/6th Track	4,000	7425	7	1	93.83 %
75	1/7th Track	4,000	6300	7	1	92.88 %

Figure 3.8.   Some examples of parameters calculated by the REXX exec of Figure 3.7.

3.4.   AN EXEC TO READ A DATASET CONTAINING NAMES OF DATASETS AND ISSUE A LISTCAT COMMAND FOR EACH

Section 4.2.4 (Figure 4.5) in Chapter 4 shows a REXX exec that will read a dataset containing fully qualified names of datasets, and issue a LISTCAT command for each. The messages produced by the LISTCAT commands will be stored in a sequential dataset.

How to use this exec. Store the exec given in Section 4.2.4 (Figure 4.5) in member DSINFO of a PDS that is allocated to DDname SYSEXEC or SYSPROC during your TSO session. To execute it, enter the following on the command line of any ISPF panel:

```
TSO %DSINFO
```

This exec will start executing. It will display the edit panel for editing member DSINFO of your PDS. (As indicated by lines 11 and 17 in the exec of Figure 4.5, the default PDS is 'prefix.PARMLIB' where prefix will be replaced by your TSO prefix when this exec is executed. You can change this PDS name if you wish.) Here you can enter the fully qualified names of datasets about which you want information, starting in column 1. So if you wanted information about datasets 'SYS3.CLIST' and 'SYS4.ISPPLIB' you would enter the following two lines:

```
SYS3.CLIST
SYS4.ISPPLIB
```

If you wanted information about n datasets, you would enter n records in this dataset. Any record that has an asterisk in column 1 will be ignored. This allows you to insert comments. When you are finished, press the key assigned to the END command (normally PF3 or PF15).

For each dataset you entered in member DSINFO, the system will first issue the WHOHAS command to display the users who might be using that dataset. (This command may be known by some other name at your installation. If you wish, you may delete line 29 from this exec, where the WHOHAS command is issued.) Then it will issue the LISTC command to display information from the MVS catalog for that dataset. The output of the LISTC command will be appended at the end of sequential file 'prefix.LISTC.PRINT' where prefix is your TSO prefix. (This dataset is deleted and then allocated in this exec. See lines 13 and 15–16.) This exec will also display on the terminal a message indicating whether or not the dataset for which it issued the LISTC command is present in the catalog. After processing all records from member DSINFO, the system will display the count of the number of datasets against which WHOHAS and LISTC commands were issued. Next the system will display the ISPF browse panel for dataset 'prefix.LISTC.PRINT', which contains output from the LISTC commands issued for all the datasets. You can browse this dataset just as you browse any other dataset using ISPF Browse. When you press the key assigned to the END command (normally PF3 or PF15), you will receive the panel where you had issued the command to execute this exec.

How does this facility work? See "How to Use This Facility to Display Information About One or More Datasets with Fully Qualified Names," Section 4.2.4 in Chapter 4. But keep in mind that in that section, exec DSINFO is invoked by entering an option on an ISPF panel, whereas in this section it was suggested above that you can also execute it directly by entering its name on any ISPF panel. This is the only difference between the two situations.

3.5. AN EXEC TO PERFORM A GLOBAL EDIT ON A PDS (CHANGE ONE STRING TO ANOTHER IN ALL MEMBERS OF THE PDS)

Suppose a TSO user has a PDS named 'prefix.JOBS.CNTL', where prefix is the user's TSO prefix. This PDS contains JCL members. The jobs have jobnames that start with the TSO user ID. Suppose this user has been promoted and his or her user ID has been changed from Z3ABC to Z2ABC. The user comes to you and asks if there is a way to change all members of his or her PDS so that all occurrences of Z3ABC will be changed to Z2ABC. *Is there a simple way to make this change?* Yes, there is, now that you have the exec shown in Figure 3.9. To use it you have to do the following:

- Copy the content of Figure 3.9 in member CHGALL of a PDS that is allocated to DDname SYSEXEC or SYSPROC during the user's TSO session.
- Copy the content of Figure 3.10 in member SAMPEM in the same PDS where you stored exec CHGALL.
- Change SAMPEM by replacing BARRY on the CHANGE command to Z3ABC and HARRY on the same line to Z2ABC. This is to tell the system to change Z3ABC to Z2ABC.

Now ask the TSO user to issue this command from the command line of any ISPF panel:

```
TSO CHGALL JOBS.CNTL SAMPEM
```

This command will invoke exec CHGALL. This exec will work on PDS 'prefix.JOBS.CNTL' where prefix will be replaced by the user's TSO prefix at execution time. It will edit each member of this PDS using the edit macro named SAMPEM, which specifies that all occurrences of Z3ABC are to be changed to Z2ABC. All members of the PDS will be changed as specified. Finally, the exec will display this message:

```
PROCESSING OF PDS JOBS.CNTL NOW COMPLETE
```

If there was any error during execution, it would display appropriate messages and then terminate.

The ISPEXEC command with options LMINIT, LMMLIST, LMOPEN, LMCLOSE, and LMFREE used in this exec are part of the library management facility of ISPF. These are described in the IBM publication *ISPF/PDF Services* (SC-34-4259). If the TRACE instruction on line 16 is uncommented, all commands in the exec will be displayed before and after they are issued. In this exec, the only command used is ISPEXEC.

```
1   /*********************** REXX **********************************/
2   /* THIS EXEC IS STORED IN MEMBER CHGALL IN A PDS THAT IS ALLOCATED TO */
3   /* DDNAME SYSEXEC OR SYSPROC. IT WILL CHANGE ALL OCCURRENCES OF ONE */
4   /* STRING INTO ANOTHER IN ALL MEMBERS OF A GIVEN PDS. IF THE DATASET */
5   /* NAME OR THE EDIT MACRO NAME WAS NOT SPECIFIED WHEN INVOKING THIS */
6   /* EXEC, THE USER WILL BE PROMPTED TO SUPPLY VALUES FOR THEM. */
7   /* EVEN THOUGH THE CODE SHOWN BELOW IS ALL IN UPPERCASE, YOU CAN */
8   /* USE LOWERCASE OR MIXEDCASE AS WELL. */
9   /* THE DATASET NAME SPECIFIED BY THE USER CAN BE FULLY-QUALIFIED WITH */
10  /* SINGLE QUOTATION MARKS, OR IT CAN BE WITHOUT QUOTATION MARKS AND */
11  /* THE PREFIX. FOR EXAMPLE: */
12  /* CHGALL PDS80A */
13  /* CHGALL 'SYS3.PROCLIB' EDITMAC */
14  /* AUTHOR: BARRY K. NIRMAL. */
15  /***************************************************************/
16  /* TRACE COMMANDS */
17  ARG DSN EMAC
18  IF DSN = '' THEN
19     DO
20        SAY 'THE DATASET NAME  PASSED TO THIS EXEC IS NULL'
21        SAY 'PLEASE ENTER THE NAME OF THE PARTITIONED DATASET'
22        SAY '(ENTERING A NULL VALUE WILL TERMINATE THIS EXEC.)'
23        PULL DSN
24        IF DSN = '' THEN
25           DO
26              SAY 'THIS EXEC IS NOW TERMINATING'
```

```
27            EXIT
28         END
29      ELSE NOP
30   END
31 ELSE NOP
32 IF EMAC = ' ' THEN
33   DO
34      SAY 'THE EDIT MACRO PASSED TO THIS EXEC IS NULL'
35      SAY 'PLEASE ENTER THE NAME OF THE EDIT MACRO'
36      SAY '(ENTERING A NULL VALUE WILL TERMINATE THIS EXEC.)'
37      PULL EMAC
38      IF EMAC = ' ' THEN
39         DO
40            SAY 'THIS EXEC IS NOW TERMINATING'
41            EXIT
42         END
43      ELSE NOP
44   END
45 ELSE NOP
46 IF SUBSTR(DSN,1,1) \= '7D'X THEN
47   DO
48      DSN  = INSERT('.',DSN,0)
49      PREF = SYSVAR(SYSPREF)
50      DSN  = INSERT(PREF,DSN,0)
51      DSN  = INSERT('7D'X,DSN,0)
52      DSN  = INSERT('7D'X,DSN,LENGTH(DSN))
```

Figure 3.9.   An exec to perform a global edit on a PDS.

continues

99

```
53     END
54   ELSE NOP
55   /***************************************************************/
56   /* AT THIS POINT, DSN CONTAINS FULLY-QUALIFIED DATASET NAME ENCLOSED */
57   /* WITHIN SINGLE QUOTATION MARKS.                                */
58   /***************************************************************/
59   LEN = LENGTH(DSN) - 2
60   DSN2 = SUBSTR(DSN,2,LEN)
61   /***************************************************************/
62   /* NOW DSN2 CONTAINS FULLY-QUALIFIED DATASET NAME BUT WITHOUT SINGLE */
63   /* QUOTATION MARKS.                                              */
64   /***************************************************************/
65   "ISPEXEC CONTROL ERRORS RETURN"
66   IF SYSDSN(DSN) \= 'OK' THEN
67     DO
68       SAY 'DATASET ' DSN ' IS NOT CATALOGED OR NOT AVAILABLE.'
69       SAY 'CHECK THIS OUT AND RERUN THIS EXEC.'
70       SAY 'THIS EXEC MET WITH AN ACCIDENT AND DIED.'
71       EXIT
72     END
73   ELSE NOP
74   "ISPEXEC LMINIT DATAID(DATAID) DATASET(""DSN"") ENQ(SHRW)",
75       " ORG(DSORG)"
76   IF DSORG \= 'PO' THEN
77     DO
78       SAY 'DATASET ' DSN ' IS NOT PARTITIONED'
79       "ISPEXEC LMFREE DATAID(""DATAID"")"
80       SAY 'THIS EXEC IS NOW TERMINATING'
```

```
81       EXIT
82     END
83   ELSE NOP
84   "ISPEXEC LMOPEN DATAID("DATAID") OPTION(INPUT)"
85   RETCODE = RC
86   DO WHILE RETCODE = 0
87     "ISPEXEC LMMLIST DATAID("DATAID") OPTION(LIST)",
88          " MEMBER(MEM)"
89     RETCODE = RC
90     IF RETCODE = 0 THEN
91       DO
92         MEM = STRIP(MEM,T)
93         "ISPEXEC EDIT DATASET('"DSN2"("MEM"')') MACRO("EMAC")"
94         ECC = RC
95         IF ECC <= 4 THEN
96           SAY 'PROCESSING  OF MEMBER ' MEM ' COMPLETE'
97         ELSE NOP
98       END
99     ELSE NOP
100  END
101  "ISPEXEC LMMLIST DATAID("DATAID") OPTION(FREE)"
102  "ISPEXEC LMCLOSE DATAID("DATAID")"
103  "ISPEXEC LMFREE DATAID("DATAID")"
104  SAY 'PROCESSING OF PDS ' DSN ' NOW COMPLETE'
105  EXIT
*********************************************************************************
```

Figure 3.9. (Continued)

```
 1  /*********************** REXX *****************************************/
 2  /* THIS IS A SAMPLE EDIT MACRO TO CHANGE ALL OCCURRENCES OF ONE STRING*/
 3  /* TO ANOTHER. IT SHOULD BE STORED IN MEMBER SAMPEM IN A PDS THAT IS  */
 4  /* ALLOCATED TO DDNAME SYSEXEC OR SYSPROC. NOTE: IF THE SOURCE STRING */
 5  /* ON THE CHANGE COMMAND CONTAINS LOWERCASE CHARACTERS, IT MAKES NO   */
 6  /* DIFFERENCE. IT WILL CHANGE THE STRING WHETHER IT IS FOUND IN LOWER-*/
 7  /* CASE, MIXEDCASE , OR UPPERCASE. BUT IF THE TARGET STRING ON THE    */
 8  /* CHANGE COMMAND CONTAINS LOWERCASE CHARACTERS, THE NEW STRING IN    */
 9  /* THE FILE WILL CONTAIN LOWERCASE CHARACTERS TOO. BUT IF THE EDIT    */
10  /* PROFILE OF A MEMBER HAS 'CAPS ON', THE RESULTANT STRING WILL BE    */
11  /* CHANGED TO CONTAIN ALL UPPERCASE CHARACTERS.                       */
12  /* IF YOU WANT TO CHANGE ANOTHER STRING, YOU CAN HAVE  A SECOND       */
13  /* ISREDIT CHANGE COMMAND. IN OTHER WORDS, MULTIPLE CHANGES CAN BE    */
14  /* MADE TO THE SAME DATASET THROUGH THIS EDIT MACRO.                  */
15  /* AUTHOR: BARRY K. NIRMAL.                                           */
16  /********************************************************************/
17  "ISREDIT MACRO"
18  "ISREDIT CHANGE ALL 'BARRY' 'HARRY' "
19  "ISREDIT BUILTIN END"
```

Figure 3.10.   An edit macro used by the exec of Figure 3.9.

3.6. AN EXEC TO DISPLAY COMPLETE INFORMATION ABOUT ANY SPECIFIED DATASET

In Figure 3.11 is a REXX exec that can be used to check if a non-VSAM dataset is cataloged, and if so, to display many lines of information about it. As stated at the beginning of this figure, it can serve as a replacement for TSO command LISTDS, which is used to display information about non-VSAM datasets.

How to use this exec. If the content of Figure 3.11 is copied in member LISTDSN of a PDS that is allocated to DDname SYSEXEC or SYSPROC during your TSO session, you can execute it by issuing the following command on the command line of any ISPF panel:

```
TSO %LISTDSN dataset-name
```

where dataset-name must be replaced by the name of the dataset about which you want information. For example, suppose you have a dataset 'prefix.JOBS.CNTL' where prefix stands for your TSO prefix (normally your TSO ID). To display information about it, enter the following command:

```
TSO %LISTDSN JOBS.CNTL
```

To display information about dataset 'SYS2.PROCLIB', enter the following command:

```
TSO %LISTDSN 'SYS2.PROCLIB'
```

If the dataset name passed to this exec is not cataloged or is not available, probably because another user has allocated it for exclusive control (DISP=OLD or DISP=MOD), it will display a message to this effect, and the following information:

- Function code from LISTDSI
- Reason code from LISTDSI
- First-level message from LISTDSI
- Second-level message from LISTDSI

```
  /****************************************** REXX ***********************************************/
1 /***************************************************************************/
2 /* THIS EXEC SHOWS HOW TO USE THE TSO/E EXTERNAL FUNCTION LISTDSI.         */
3 /* IT WILL DISPLAY INFORMATION ABOUT ANY NON-VSAM DATASET YOU SPECIFY.     */
4 /* IT CAN BE USED IN THE PLACE OF IBM-SUPPLIED LISTDS COMMAND.             */
5 /***************************************************************************/
6 ARG DSN
7 IF SUBSTR(DSN,1,1) \= '7D'X THEN
8   DO
9     DSN = INSERT('.',DSN,0)
10    PREF = SYSVAR(SYSPREF)
11    DSN = INSERT(PREF,DSN,0)
12    DSN = INSERT('7D'X.DSN.0)
13    DSN = INSERT('7D'X,DSN,LENGTH(DSN))
14  END
15 ELSE NOP
16 /***************************************************************************/
17 /* AT THIS POINT DSN CONTAINS FULLY-QUALIFIED DATASET NAME ENCLOSED        */
18 /* WITHIN SINGLE QUOTATION MARKS.                                         */
19 /***************************************************************************/
20 X = LISTDSI(DSN)
21 IF X \= 0  THEN
22   DO
23     SAY 'DATASET ' DSN ' IS NOT CATALOGED OR NOT AVAILABLE. '
24     SAY '----------------------------------------------------'
```

```
25    SAY 'FUNCTION CODE RETURNED BY LISTDSI IS ' X
26    SAY ' ( 0 = NORMAL COMPLETION     )'
27    SAY ' ( 4 = SOME DATASET INFO IS UNAVAILABLE)'
28    SAY ' (16 = SEVERE ERROR OCCURRED)'
29    SAY '-----------------------------------------------'
30    SAY 'REASON CODE   RETURNED BY LISTDSI IS ' SYSREASON
31    SAY 'FIRST LEVEL MESSAGE FROM LISTDSE IS ' SYSMSGLVL1
32    SAY 'SECOND LEVEL MESAGE FROM LISTDSI IS ' SYSMSGLVL2
33    SAY 'CORRECT THIS ERROR AND RETRY'
34    EXIT
35    END
36    SAY 'DATASET NAME -------------------------------->' SYSDSNAME
37    SAY 'VOLUME SERIAL ID ---------------------------->' SYSVOLUME
38    SAY 'DEVICE UNIT ON WHICH THIS VOLUME RESIDES ------->' SYSUNIT
39    SAY 'DATASET ORGANIZATION ------------------------->' SYSDSORG
40    SAY 'RECORD FORMAT -------------------------------->' SYSRECFM
41    SAY 'LOGICAL RECORD LENGTH ------------------------>' SYSLRECL
42    SAY 'BLOCK SIZE ----------------------------------->' SYSBLKSIZE
43    SAY 'KEY LENGTH ----------------------------------->' SYSKEYLEN
44    SAY 'ALLOCATION IN SPACE UNITS -------------------->' SYSALLOC
45    SAY 'ALLOCATION USED IN SPACE UNITS --------------->' SYSUSED
46    SAY 'PRIMARY ALLOCATION IN SPACE UNITS ------------>' SYSPRIMARY
47    SAY 'SECONDARY ALLOCATION IN SPACE UNITS ---------->' SYSSECONDS
48    SAY 'SPACE UNITS ---------------------------------->' SYSUNITS
49    SAY 'NUMBER OF EXTENTS USED ----------------------->' SYSEXTENTS
```

Figure 3.11.   An exec that shows how to use the LISTDSI function.   *continues*

```
50  SAY  'CREATION DATE ---------------------------------------->'  SYSCREATE
51  SAY  'LAST REFERENCE DATE ---------------------------------->'  SYSREFDATE
52  SAY  'EXPIRATION DATE -------------------------------------->'  SYSEXDATE
53  SAY  'PASSWORD INDICATION ---------------------------------->'  SYSPASSWORD
54  SAY  'RACF INDICATION -------------------------------------->'  SYSRACFA
55  SAY  'UPDATE INDICATOR (FILE HAS BEEN UPDATED OR NOT) ------>'  SYSUPDATED
56  SAY  'TRACKS PER CYLINDER FOR THE UNIT DISPLAYED ABOVE ----->'  SYSTRKSCYL
57  SAY  'BLOCKS PER TRACK FOR THE UNIT DISPLAYED ABOVE -------->'  SYSBLKSTRK
58  SAY  'DIR BLOCKS ALLOCATED IF DATASET IS PARTITIONED ------->'  SYSADIRBLK
59  SAY  'DIR BLOCKS USED IF DATASET IS PARTITIONED ------------>'  SYSUDIRBLK
60  SAY  'NUMBER OF MEMBERS IF DATASET IS PARTITIONED --------->'   SYSMEMBERS
61  SAY  '-------------------------------------------------------'
62  SAY  '(DIRECTORY BLOCKS ALLOCATED AND USED, AND NUMBER OF MEMBERS ARE'
63  SAY  ' RETUREND ONLY WHEN A DATASET IS PARTITIONED AND DIRECTORY IS'
64  SAY  ' SPECIFIED WHEN ISSUING THE LISTDSI FUNCTION.)'
65  EXIT
```

****

Figure 3.11.   (Continued)

These will help you in ascertaining the cause of the error. See Appendix D for the meaning of the function codes and the reason codes set by LISTDSI. This appendix also gives the meanings of all the variables set by LISTDSI that are displayed in Figure 3.11.

3.7.   AN EXEC TO CHECK IF A DATASET OR A PDS MEMBER EXISTS

Figure 3.12 shows a REXX exec that can be used to determine if a dataset or a PDS member exists and is available. To use it, copy the content of this figure in member DETDS of a PDS that is allocated to DDname SYSEXEC or SYSPROC during your TSO session. Now you can invoke it by issuing the following command from the command line of any ISPF panel:

```
TSO %DETDS dataset-name
            or
TSO %DETDS PDS-member-name
```

For example, suppose you want to check if dataset 'SYS3.CLIST' exists and is available. You can issue this command:

```
TSO %DETDS 'SYS3.CLIST'
```

Suppose your TSO prefix is RF. To check if dataset 'RF.LIB.LOAD' exists, issue this command:

```
TSO %DETDS LIB.LOAD
```

Suppose 'SYS3.CLIST' is a PDS. You want to check if it contains member CALC. You can issue the following command:

```
TSO %DETDS 'SYS3.CLIST(CALC)'
```

This exec uses TSO external function SYSDSN to determine the availability of a dataset. On line 16 in Figure 3.12, we have

```
X = SYSDSN(DSN)
```

```
   /**************** REXX ******************************/
1  /* THIS EXEC WILL CHECK IF A DATASET OR A PDS MEMBER IS CATALOGED */
2  /* AND AVAILABLE.                                     */
3  /* AUTHOR: BARRY KUMAR NIRMAL                         */
4  /****************************************************/
5
6  PARSE ARG DSN
7  IF SUBSTR(DSN,1,1) \= '7D'X THEN
8    DO
9      DSN = INSERT('.',DSN,0)
10     PREF = SYSVAR(SYSPREF)
11     DSN = INSERT(PREF,DSN,0)
12     DSN = INSERT('7D'X,DSN,0)
13     DSN = INSERT('7D'X,DSN,LENGTH(DSN))
14   END
15 ELSE NOP
16 X = SYSDSN(DSN)
17 SAY 'THE STATUS OF FILE: ' DSN ' IS ' X
18 IF X = 'OK' THEN RETURN 0
19 ELSE IF X = 'UNAVAILABLE DATASET' THEN RETURN 1
20 ELSE RETURN 2
21 EXIT
   /****************************************************/
```

Figure 3.12. An exec showing how to use the SYSDSN function.

So the content of variable DSN will be passed to SYSDSN. This function will place OK in X if the dataset exists and is available, or else it will place one of the following messages in variable X:

```
MEMBER SPECIFIED, BUT DATASET IS NOT PARTITIONED
MEMBER NOT FOUND
DATASET NOT FOUND
ERROR PROCESSING REQUESTED DATASET
PROTECTED DATASET
VOLUME NOT ON SYSTEM
UNAVAILABLE DATASET
INVALID DATASET NAME, dataset-name
MISSING DATASET NAME
```

This exec also sets a return code before terminating. The return code will be zero if the dataset or PDS member exists and is available. It will be 1 if the dataset is unavailable, meaning that probably some other user is allocating it for exclusive control (DISP=OLD or DISP=MOD). It will be 2 in other situations. The exec given in Figure 2.18 in Chapter 2 that copies a sequential file into another uses the exec shown in Figure 3.12. That exec utilizes the capability of this exec to set a return code. See Figure 2.18 to understand how it checks the return code set by Figure 3.12.

3.8.   AN EXEC TO SCAN ALL MEMBERS OF A PDS FOR ANY SPECIFIED STRING

In Figure 3.13 is an exec that can be used to scan all members of any partitioned dataset for any string. The PDS can have any record length.

How to use this exec. Read the comments in the beginning of this exec; they explain how to use it. If this exec is stored in member SCANPDS of a partitioned dataset that is allocated to DDname SYSEXEC or SYSPROC during your TSO session, you can invoke it by simply entering the following on the command line of any ISPF panel:

```
TSO SCANPDS
```

```rexx
     /****************** REXX ******************/
1    /****************** REXX ******************/
2    /* THIS IS A COMMAND TO SCAN ALL MEMBERS OF A PARTITIONED DATASET FOR */
3    /* THE PRESENCE OF ANY SPECIFIED STRING. FOR EXAMPLE, TO SCAN PDS     */
4    /* 'SYS2.PROCLIB' FOR STRING CICS170A, ISSUE THE FOLLOWING COMMAND:   */
5    /*                                                                    */
6    /*     TSO SCANPDS 'SYS2.PROCLIB' CICS170A                            */
7    /*                                                                    */
8    /* THE DATASET NAME SPECIFIED ON THE COMMAND CAN BE FULLY OR PARTIALLY*/
9    /* QUALIFIED. IF FULLY-QUALIFIED, IT MUST BE ENCLOSED WITHIN SINGLE   */
10   /* QUOTATION MARKS. THIS RULE IS THE SAME AS WHEN ISSUING ANY TSO     */
11   /* COMMAND SUCH AS LISTDS AND LISTC.                                  */
12   /* AUTHOR: BARRY K. NIRMAL                                            */
13   /****************** ... ******************/
14   /* TRACE COMMAND  */
15   ARG PDS STRING .
16   IF PDS = '' THEN
17     DO
18       SAY 'THE PDS NAME  PASSED TO THIS EXEC IS NULL'
19       SAY 'PLEASE ENTER THE NAME OF THE PARTITIONED DATASET'
20       SAY '(ENTERING A NULL VALUE WILL TERMINATE THIS EXEC.)'
21       PULL PDS
22       IF PDS = '' THEN
23         DO
24           SAY 'THIS EXEC IS NOW TERMINATING'
25           EXIT
26         END
27       ELSE NOP
```

```
28       END
29    ELSE NOP
30    IF STRING = '' THEN
31       DO
32          SAY 'THE STRING PASSED TO THIS EXEC IS NULL'
33          SAY 'PLEASE ENTER THE STRING YOU WANT SEARCHED'
34          SAY '(ENTERING A NULL VALUE WILL TERMINATE THIS EXEC.)'
35          PULL STRING
36          IF STRING = '' THEN
37             DO
38                SAY 'THIS EXEC IS NOW TERMINATING'
39                EXIT
40             END
41          ELSE NOP
42       END
43    ELSE NOP
44    IF SUBSTR(PDS,1,1) \= '7D'X THEN
45       DO
46          PDS  = INSERT('.',PDS,0)
47          PREF = SYSVAR(SYSPREF)
48          PDS  = INSERT(PREF,PDS,0)
49          PDS  = INSERT('7D'X,PDS,0)
50          PDS  = INSERT('7D'X,PDS,LENGTH(PDS))
51       END
52    ELSE NOP
```

Figure 3.13. An exec to scan all members of a PDS for any specified string.

continues

111

```
53  /*******************************************************/
54  /* AT THIS POINT, PDS CONTAINS FULLY-QUALIFIED DATASET NAME ENCLOSED */
55  /* WITHIN SINGLE QUOTATION MARKS.                      */
56  /*******************************************************/
57  LEN = LENGTH(PDS) - 2
58  PDS2 = SUBSTR(PDS,2,LEN)
59  SAY 'SEARCHING ' PDS ' FOR STRING ' STRING
60  /*******************************************************/
61  /* NOW PDS2 CONTAINS FULLY-QUALIFIED DATASET NAME BUT WITHOUT SINGLE */
62  /* QUOTATION MARKS.                                    */
63  /*******************************************************/
64  MEM_COUNT = 0
65  X = OUTTRAP("VAR.")
66  "LISTDS "PDS" MEMBERS "
67  MEM_COUNT = VAR.0 - 7 + 1
68  /* SAY 'NUMBER OF LINES TRAPPED DUE TO THE LISTDS COMMAND= ' VAR.0    */
69  /*******************************************************/
70  /* IF PDS HAS NO MEMBER, VAR.0 WILL BE 6, AND MEM_COUNT WILL BE ZERO. */
71  /* IN THIS CASE, THE FOLLOWING DO LOOP WILL NOT BE EXECUTED EVEN ONCE.*/
72  /*******************************************************/
73  DO I = 7 TO VAR.0
74      MEM_NAME = SUBSTR(VAR.I,3,8)
75      MEM_NAME = STRIP(MEM_NAME,T)
76      CALL SCANMEM
77  END
78  SAY 'PROCESSING OF PDS ' PDS ' WITH ' MEM_COUNT ' MEMBERS COMPLETED'
79  EXIT
80  /*****THE FOLLOWING IS AN INTERNAL SUBROUTINE *********************/
81  SCANMEM:
82  SAY 'PROCESSING OF MEMBER ' MEM_NAME ' STARTING'
```

```
83   RECNUM = 0
84   /**************************************************************/
85   /* THE REUSE OPERAND ON THE ALLOC COMMAND ENSURES THAT EVEN IF DDNAME */
86   /* MYFILE IS ALREADY ALLOCATED, THE ALLOC COMMAND WILL NOT FAIL, I.E. */
87   /* IT WILL NOT END IN CONDITION CODE 12.                      */
88   /**************************************************************/
89   /* NOTE: EVEN IF A TSO USER IS EDITING A MEMBER OF THE PDS BEING    */
90   /* SCANNED, THIS EXEC WILL FUNCTION PROPERLY. BUT THE CONTENT OF THE */
91   /* MEMBER BEING EDITED THAT IS READ BY THIS EXEC WILL BE THE ONE THAT */
92   /* WAS LAST SAVED. THIS IS TO SAY THAT ANY CHANGE MADE TO THE MEMBER */
93   /* BY THE TSO USER ON THE ISPF EDIT PANEL WILL NOT BE REPORTED.   */
94   /**************************************************************/
95   "ALLOC F(MYFILE) DA('"PDS2"("MEM_NAME")') SHR REUSE"
96   RETCODE = RC
97   IF RETCODE \= 0 THEN
98      DO
99      SAY 'AN ERROR OCCURRED IN ALLOCATING THE FOLLOWING DATASET:'
100     SAY PDS2'('MEM_NAME')'
101     SAY 'THE RETURN CODE FROM THE ALLOC COMMAND WAS:' RETCODE
102     SAY 'PLEASE INVESTIGATE THIS PROBLEM, CORRECT THE ERROR AND RETRY'
103     SAY 'THIS EXEC MET WITH AN ACCIDENT AND DIED IN A HURRY'
104     EXIT
105     END
106  ELSE NOP
107  FINITO = 'NO'
```

Figure 3.13.   *continues*

113

```
108   DO WHILE FINITO = 'NO'
109   "EXECIO 1 DISKR MYFILE "
110   IF RC = 0 THEN
111       DO
112           PULL RECORD
113           RECNUM = RECNUM + 1
114           IF INDEX(RECORD,STRING) \= 0 THEN
115               DO
116                   SAY 'YOUR STRING WAS FOUND IN RECORD NUMBER' RECNUM,
117                       'WHICH IS AS FOLLOWS'
118                   SAY RECORD
119               END
120           ELSE NOP
121       END
122   ELSE FINITO = 'YES'
123   END
124   "EXECIO 0 DISKR MYFILE (FINIS "        /* CLOSE THE FILE */
125   RETURN
```
****

Figure 3.13.   (Continued)

114

It will prompt you for the PDS name, which you can enter as partially or fully qualified. If you entered a null string for the PDS name, that is, if you simply pressed Enter without typing anything, the exec will terminate. Then it will prompt you for the string to be searched. Again, if you entered a null string, it will terminate. If the PDS name and the string to be searched are not null, it uses the OUTTRAP function on line 65 to specify that messages from commands be stored in compound variables VAR.1, VAR.2, and so on, and the total number of message lines be stored in VAR.0. Then on line 66 it issues the LISTDS command with MEMBERS option to list the member names of the specified PDS. Then in the DO loop started on line 73 and ended on line 77, it stores each member name in variable MEM_NAME and then calls internal subroutine SCANMEM. After processing all members, it displays the number of members processed on line 78 and on line 79 it terminates.

Now let us see what happens in the internal subroutine started on line 81. This subroutine returns to the caller through the RETURN instruction on line 125. On line 95 we allocate the PDS member being processed to DDname MYFILE. Then we read each record of the PDS member as if it was a sequential file. (The EXECIO command on line 109 reads one record from the file.) We scan each record for the specified string. (The INDEX built-in function is used on line 114 to check if the record contains the string contained in variable STRING.) If the string is found, on lines 116–118 we display both the record number and the record itself. When all records have been processed from the PDS member, the EXECIO command on line 124 closes the sequential file, and the RETURN instruction on line 125 returns control to the caller.

3.8.1.   How Can This Exec Be Useful to the IS Professionals?

This exec can be of great help to every programmer and analyst, especially in applications programming. Some MVS shops have an Assembler program that is used to scan a PDS for any specified string. This exec can be used in the place of such an Assembler program. As you can see, this exec is easy to understand and modify. Few people have the expertise to support Assembler programs. But the skill needed to modify and support REXX execs can be easily acquired, especially now that you have this and other books on REXX.

This exec also shows how to use the OUTTRAP function. Because of the use of OUTTRAP on line 65, the output lines produced by the LISTDS command on line 66 are stored in compound variables VAR.1, VAR.2, and so on, and the count of output lines are stored in VAR.0. Since the first member name is on output line 7, on line 73 we specify 7 as the starting value and VAR.0 as the ending value for I. In addition, because member name starts in column 3 of the output line, we use 3 as the starting position on the SUBSTR function on line 74. And since member name can be at the most 8 characters long, we specify 8 as the length on the SUBSTR function on line 74.

3.9. AN EXEC SHOWING HOW TO USE THE DATA STACK TO PASS INFORMATION TO AN EXTERNAL SUBROUTINE

Here are two execs that can be used to define any non-VSAM dataset with the same characteristics as an existing one. These execs also show

- how to write an external subroutine
- how to place one or more items on the data stack for retrieval by the external subroutine

The exec of Figure 3.14 places two items on the data stack using the QUEUE instruction. This means that the items will go in the stack in FIFO, that is, First In, First Out, order. (Note: If you use the PUSH instruction to place items on the data stack, they are placed in the LIFO, that is, Last In, First Out, order.) Figure 3.16 (below) depicts these rules better than words can.

How does this exec work? Suppose the exec of Figure 3.14 is stored in member ALLOCDSN and that of Figure 3.15 in member ALLOCNEW of a PDS that is allocated to DDname SYSEXEC or

SYSPROC during your TSO session. You can invoke ALLOCNEW by entering the following on any ISPF panel:

```
TSO %ALLOCDSN
```

It will prompt you to enter the old dataset name. You will be prompted again if you entered a null value, that is, if you simply pressed the Enter key without entering anything. If you entered only a question mark, it will display a number of explanatory messages. If you entered Q, the exec will terminate. (This is to allow you to quit if you executed this exec by mistake, or if you changed your mind. *Every well-designed system or program provides the user with such escape routes.*) Next, it will prompt you to enter the new dataset name. It will prompt you again if you entered a null value, that is, if you simply pressed the Enter key without entering anything. If you entered only a question mark, it will display a number of explanatory messages. If you entered Q, it will terminate.

If you entered old and new dataset names correctly, it will place the old dataset name and then the new dataset name on the data stack using the QUEUE instruction. Then it will call the external subroutine named ALLOCNEW, shown in Figure 3.15. This subroutine will first fetch the old dataset name and then the new dataset name from the data stack using the PULL instruction. (Remember, as shown by Figure 3.16, elements can be placed either on top or at the bottom of the data stack, but the removal of elements from the data stack occurs always from the top.) It will then issue the ALLOC command to allocate the new dataset name using the LIKE operand. As explained in the comments at the bottom of Figure 3.15, the return code from the ALLOC command is passed back to the caller on the RETURN instruction. The caller then checks the value in special variable RESULT. If it contains zero, it displays the message that the allocation was successful, or else it displays the message that allocation failed.

```
01  /********************** REXX *******************************/
02  /* This exec shows how to place information in the data     */
03  /* stack for use by an external subroutine. This exec       */
04  /* allows you to allocate another dataset with the same     */
05  /* characteristics as an existing one.                      */
06  /* Author: Barry K. Nirmal                                  */
07  /**********************************************************/
08  MSG1 = 'This REXX exec allows you to allocate a new ',
09  'non-VSAM dataset with the same characteristics as an ',
10  'existing dataset. You will be prompted to enter the names of',
11  'old and new datasets.'
12  MSG2 = 'In MVS dataset name can be specified',
13  'either as fully-qualified or without the first qualifier.',
14  'When you enclose the dataset name within single quotation',
15  'marks, it is considered fully-qualified. When you leave ',
16  'out the single quotation marks, the system adds your prefix',
17  'in the beginning of the name you provide, as its first',
18  'qualifier.'
19  MSG3 = 'Your TSO prefix is normally, but not necessarily',
20  'the same as your TSO ID. A new dataset name can not be the',
21  'same as an existing dataset name. Now enter the dataset name',
22  'please (old or new depending on what was asked earlier)....'
23  S = 'To obtain help, please enter ?. To quit, enter Q.'
24  old_dsn = ''
25  Do while old_dsn = ''
```

```
26      Say 'Enter the old dataset name please.'
27      Say S
28      Pull old_dsn
29      End
30      dsn = old_dsn
31      Call check_dsn
32      old_dsn = dsn
33      new_dsn = ''
34      Do while new_dsn = ''
35         Say 'Enter the new dataset name please.'
36         Say S
37         Pull new_dsn
38      End
39      dsn = new_dsn
40      Call check_dsn
41      new_dsn = dsn
42      Queue old_dsn
43      Queue new_dsn
44      Call Allocnew              /* Call the external subroutine */
45      If Result > 0 Then
46         Say 'An error occurred while allocating ' new_dsn
```

Figure 3.14. A REXX exec that will allocate a new dataset with the same characteristics as an existing dataset.

continues

119

```
47    Else
48      Say 'Your dataset ' new_dsn ' has been successfully allocated'
49    EXIT
50    /****** The following is an internal subroutine. ********/
51    Check_dsn:
52    DO while dsn = '?'
53      SAY MSG1
54      SAY MSG2
55      SAY MSG3
56      Say S
57      Pull dsn
58    END
59    If dsn = 'Q' Then
60      Exit
61    Else NOP
62    Return
```

Figure 3.14. (Continued)

```
01  /****************** REXX ******************************/
02  /* This external subroutine removes the old and new data  */
03  /* set names placed on the data stack by the exec of      */
04  /* Figure 3.14. It then allocates the new dataset. This    */
05  /* exec also returns a code which the caller can check.    */
06  /* Author: Barry K. Nirmal                                 */
07  /********************************************************/
08  Pull old_file_name
09  Pull new_file_name
10  "Allocate da("new_file_name") new like("old_file_name")"
11  /********************************************************/
12  /* The ALLOC command sets a return code in special variable */
13  /* RC. On the RETURN instruction below, we use the same    */
14  /* variable. The caller can check the return code to know  */
15  /* if the ALLOC command was successful. A value of zero    */
16  /* means no error.                                         */
17  /********************************************************/
18  Return RC
```

Figure 3.15. The external subroutine ALLOCNEW called by the REXX exec of Figure 3.14.

121

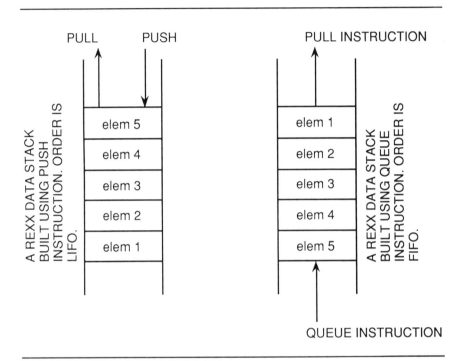

Figure 3.16. Depiction of how PUSH, PULL, and QUEUE instructions work in REXX.

3.10. AN EXEC SHOWING HOW TO USE THE DATA STACK TO STORE COMMANDS FOR EXECUTION AFTER THE EXEC ENDS

The exec shown in Figure 3.17 shows how to place some commands on the data stack for execution after the exec has ended. When a REXX exec ends, any items remaining on the stack are pulled off and executed as TSO commands. If an item is not a valid command, including explicit or implicit invocation of a CLIST or REXX exec, the user receives the message to this effect.

Let us see what this exec does. If it is stored in member LOCKTERM of a PDS that is allocated to DDname SYSEXEC or SYSPROC during your TSO session, you can invoke it by entering the following command on any ISPF panel:

```
01  /******************************* REXX ***********************************/
02  /* This exec shows how to store some commands on the REXX */
03  /* data stack. These commands will be executed after the */
04  /* exec terminates.                                       */
05  /* Author: Barry K. Nirmal                                */
06  /************************************************************************/
07  EXEC_NAME = SYSVAR(SYSICMD)
08  IF EXEC_NAME = ' ' THEN
09      DO
10          SAY 'THIS EXEC WAS NOT EXECUTED IMPLICITLY.'
11          SAY 'HENCE THIS EXEC IS TERMINATING ABNORMALLY.'
12          EXIT
13      END
14  ELSE NOP
15  SAY 'ENTER THE PASSWORD TO UNLOCK THIS TERMINAL:'
16  PULL PWD
17  IF PWD = 'QED/USA' THEN
18      SAY 'YOUR PASSWORD IS CORRECT. THIS TERMINAL IS NOW FREE.'
19  ELSE
20      DO
21          QUEUE "SEND 'YOU ARE A GREAT PERSON.' USER(*) "
22          QUEUE "TIME"
23          QUEUE '%'EXEC_NAME
24      END
25  EXIT
```

Figure 3.17. A REXX exec that can be used to lock your terminal.

123

```
TSO %LOCKTERM
```

It will prompt you to enter the password for unlocking the terminal. If you enter the correct password (QED/USA) in lower, upper, or mixed case, it will display a message saying that your password is correct, and then it will terminate. However, if the password is not correct, it will use the QUEUE instruction to add the following commands on the data stack:

```
SEND 'YOU ARE A GREAT PERSON.' USER(*)
TIME
%LOCKTERM
```

Then it will terminate. The system will then fetch the items from the data stack and execute them as TSO commands. First the SEND command will be fetched from the stack. (See Figure 3.16, which explains how the QUEUE instruction places items on the stack in FIFO order.) The SEND command will send the following message to the same user who was using this exec (you):

```
YOU ARE A GREAT PERSON.
```

This is due to USER(*) on the SEND command. Next the TIME command will be executed. It will display the current time and date on the terminal. The next command is an implicit execution of this same exec, so this exec will again be executed. It will again prompt you for the password, and the process described above will be repeated.

How does this exec know its own name? On line 7 it uses the SYSVAR function with the argument SYSICMD to determine the name by which it was implicitly invoked. If it was invoked explicitly, the value returned by SYSVAR will be null. So, for example, if you issued this command to execute it:

```
TSO EX 'PDS-name(LOCKTERM)' EX
```

it will display the message saying that this exec was not executed implicitly; hence this exec is terminating abnormally.

3.10.1. How Can This Exec Be Useful to You?

If you are going away from your desk for some time, you may execute it to lock your terminal. It will prompt for the password. If someone comes to your terminal and enters a wrong password, this exec will reject it and prompt him or her again. In effect, your terminal has been locked. But you have to consider that the intruder who is trying to use your terminal may press an attention key, that is, ATTN or PA1, to terminate the exec. If he or she pressed the PA1 key, the system would display the following message:

```
ENTER HI TO END, A NULL LINE TO CONTINUE,
OR AN IMMEDIATE COMMAND+
```

At this point, the intruder can enter HI to terminate this exec. (HI stands for Halt Interpretation.) You are advised to talk to someone in the technical support division of your information systems department who knows about TSO, and insert the necessary code in Figure 3.17 so that even if the user pressed PA1 or ATTN, he or she would not be able to terminate this exec.

3.11. A FACILITY FOR EXTENDED EDIT/BROWSE UNDER ISPF

Most of the programmers and analysts who work with TSO spend a large portion of their time editing or browsing a variety of datasets. These datasets are usually sequential or partitioned. If they had a facility that would quicken the edit/browse process, it would go a long way toward increasing their productivity. As you know, the normal ISPF edit and browse panels allow you to enter only one library name or nonstandard dataset name on the edit or browse entry panel. Here is a facility that has the following strong points:

1. It allows you to enter multiple dataset names on the panel and select any one of them for edit or browse. It also remembers the dataset names you had entered before and the particular dataset number that you had selected last time. This way you can enter the names of datasets you commonly use

only once. The system will remember them for you and display them on the browse/edit entry panel whenever it is displayed.
2. There is only one panel where you specify whether you want to edit a dataset or browse it. This way you don't have to use two panels, one for edit and another for browse.
3. It illustrates the technique of developing user-friendly online facilities using ISPF panels and REXX execs.
4. It shows how to use the VALUE built-in function of REXX to dynamically build the name of a variable and fetch its content.

The components of this system are shown in Figures 3.18 through 3.20 (below). First let us see how to install it. We will then discuss using it.

3.11.1.   Procedure for Installing This Facility

Step 1. Copy the panel shown in Figure 3.18 in member XEDTBRO of a partitioned dataset that is usually allocated to DDname ISPPLIB during your TSO session. To explain this point, suppose your TSO prefix is Z1BKN and during your TSO session, DDname ISPPLIB is allocated to many datasets, one of which is Z1BKN.ISPPLIB. (To find out the datasets allocated to ISPPLIB, issue this command from the command line of any ISPF panel:

```
TSO LISTA ST H
```

This will show you not only ISPPLIB but all the other DDnames that are currently allocated.)

In member XEDTBRO of Z1BKN.ISPPLIB, you can copy the content of Figure 3.18.

Step 2. Copy the panel shown in Figure 3.19 in member XHELP of the same partitioned dataset in which you created member XEDTBRO in Step 1 above.

Step 3. Copy the REXX exec shown in Figure 3.20 in member XEDTBRO of a partitioned dataset that contains REXX execs or CLISTs and that is allocated to DDname SYSEXEC or SYSPROC during your TSO session. Again, to find out the datasets allocated to SYSEXEC or SYSPROC, issue this command from the command line of any ISPF panel:

```
TSO LISTA ST H
```

This will show you not only SYSEXEC but also all the other DDnames that are currently allocated. Suppose you find that Z1BKN.EXEC is allocated to DDname SYSEXEC and that Z1BKN.CLIST is allocated to DDname SYSPROC. You can copy Figure 3.20 in member XEDTBRO of Z1BKN.EXEC or Z1BKN.CLIST.

3.11.2. How to Display the Extended Edit/Browse Panel

There are three methods of displaying and using the panel shown in Figure 3.18.

Method 1. From the command line of any ISPF panel, enter the following command:

```
TSO %XEDTBRO
```

This will display the panel shown in Figure 3.18. On this panel, leave the command line blank, and enter E in the action field and a dataset number to edit that dataset, or enter B in the action field and a dataset number to browse it. On the browse or edit panel thus received, when you press the PF key associated with the END command (normally PF3 or PF15), you will receive the extended edit/browse panel. And when you press the END key on the extended edit/browse panel, you will receive the panel where you had entered the XEDTBRO command.

Method 2. If you enter the REXX exec of Figure 3.20 as a command in your ISPF command table, you can pop in and out of extended edit/browse from any other ISPF panel. Suppose you add it to the command table under name EXT; then, on the command line of any ISPF panel, you can simply enter EXT to invoke this exec and obtain the panel shown in Figure 3.18. Read Sec-

```
)ATTR
  %  TYPE(TEXT)    INTENS(HIGH)
  +  TYPE(TEXT)    INTENS(LOW) SKIP(ON)
  _  TYPE(INPUT)   INTENS(LOW)    JUST(LEFT) PAD(' ') CAPS(ON)
  $  TYPE(INPUT)   INTENS(HIGH)   JUST(LEFT) PAD(' ') CAPS(ON)
  #  TYPE(OUTPUT)  INTENS(HIGH) JUST(LEFT) PAD(' ') CAPS(OFF)
)BODY
%----  EXTENDED EDIT/ BROWSE FACILITY --(PF1/13 HELP) #SAVE
%COMMAND --->_ZCMD
+
+ EDIT OR BROWSE ? (E= EDIT, B= BROWSE) ------------> $F       +
+ DATASET NUMBER TO BE BROWSED/EDITED      ----------> $SEQ    +
+
%          DATASET NAME (MAX 44 CHARACTERS)                          DATASET NAME
%        <-------------------------------->                      <----------------------->+
  1%=>_NDSN1                                          +16%=>_NDSN16                       +
  2%=>_NDSN2                                          +17%=>_NDSN17                       +
  3%=>_NDSN3                                          +18%=>_NDSN18                       +
  4%=>_NDSN4                                          ÷19%=>_NDSN19                       +
  5%=>_NDSN5                                          +20%=>_NDSN20                       +
  6%=>_NDSN6                                          +21%=>_NDSN21                       +
  7%=>_NDSN7                                          +22%=>_NDSN22                       +
```

```
8%=>_NDSN8                                                  +23%=>_NDSN23    +
9%=>_NDSN9                                                  +24%=>_NDSN24    +
10%=>_NDSN10                                                +25%=>_NDSN25    +
11%=>_NDSN11                                                +26%=>_NDSN26    +
12%=>_NDSN12                                                +27%=>_NDSN27    +
13%=>_NDSN13                                                +28%=>_NDSN28    +
14%=>_NDSN14                                                +29%=>_NDSN29    +
15%=>_NDSN15                                                +30%=>_NDSN30    +
+
)INIT
&F = &Z
.CURSOR = F
.HELP = XHELP
)PROC
VER(&F,NB)
VER(&F,LIST,E,B)
VER(&SEQ,NB)
VER(&SEQ,LIST,1,2,3,4,5,6,7,8,9,10,11,12,13,14,15,16,17,18
    19,20,21,22,23,24,25,26,27,28,29,30)

&CMD = TRUNC (&ZCMD,'.')
VPUT (NDSN1,NDSN2,NDSN3,NDSN4,NDSN5,NDSN6,NDSN7,NDSN8,NDSN9,NDSN10,
      NDSN11,NDSN12,NDSN13,NDSN14,NDSN15,NDSN16,NDSN17,NDSN18,NDSN19,
      NDSN20,NDSN21,NDSN22,NDSN23,NDSN24,NDSN25,NDSN26,NDSN27,NDSN28,
      NDSN29,NDSN30,SEQ) PROFILE

)END
```

Figure 3.18.   Extended edit/browse panel.

tion 6.6 in Chapter 6 to learn how the ISPF command table works and how to add a REXX exec or a CLIST to the ISPF command table.

Method 3. You need to determine the dataset containing your primary ISPF panel. Suppose your TSO prefix is Z1BKN and your primary ISPF panel is in Z1BKN.ISPPLIB(ISR@PRIM). You can modify this panel by inserting option E as follows:

```
%  E + Extended Edit/ Browse Facility
```

(If option E is being used for some other task, you can choose some other letter. Then, in the lower part of the file where normally there is one line for handling each option, you can insert a line as follows to handle option E:

```
E,'CMD(XEDTBRO)'
```

When you select option E on your ISPF primary menu, you will receive the extended edit/browse panel, provided the panels of Figures 3.18 and 3.19 have been copied in members XEDTBRO and XHELP, respectively, of a PDS that is allocated to DDname ISPPLIB during your TSO session.

Once you have obtained the extended edit/browse panel, using it is easy. Figure 3.18 shows the valid options. The main thing to remember is that once you have entered the names of commonly used datasets on this panel, the system will remember them, and the next time you access extended edit/extended browse, the dataset names entered or modified during the last use will be displayed on the panel.

On the extended edit/browse panel, when you press the PF key associated with the HELP command (normally PF1 or PF15), you will receive the panel shown in Figure 3.19. On the help panel, the only field that is open for input is on the command line. On the help panel, press the END key to return to the extended edit/ browse panel. On the panels of Figures 3.18 and 3.19, you can enter any valid TSO command on the command line to execute that command. For example, on each of the two panels, you can

```
)BODY
-------- EXTENDED EDIT/ BROWSE FACILITY - HELP PANEL ----------&TIME
-COMMAND ---> _ZCMD
+
+ EDIT OR BROWSE ? (E= EDIT, B= BROWSE) -------> E
+ DATASET NUMBER TO BE BROWSED/EDITED    -------> 2
+
-      DATASET NAME (MAX 44 CHARACTERS)                   DATASET NAME
-    <-----------------------------------------> <------------------------------------------>+
1-=> ISPPLIB(ISR@PRIM)                       +16-=>CLIST                                      +
2-=> 'SYS2.PROCLIB'                          +17-=>PDS.DOC(PRINT)                             +
+
+ THE EXTENDED EDIT/BROWSE FACILITY ALLOWS YOU TO SPECIFY UP TO 30
+ DATASETS ON THE PANEL. THE NAMES OF THESE DATASETS WILL BE REMEMBERED
+ SO THAT THE NEXT TIME YOU DISPLAY THIS PANEL, THEY WILL BE PRESENT.
+ THIS WILL ALLOW YOU TO SELECT ANY DATASET FOR EDIT OR BROWSE.
+
+ IN THE DATASET NAME YOU MAY OR MAY NOT USE SINGLE QUOTES. IF SINGLE
+ QUOTES ARE NOT USED, YOUR TSO PREFIX WILL BE ADDED AS THE FIRST
+ QUALIFIER OF THE DATASET. THE DATASET NUMBER IS ALSO SAVED ACROSS
+ SESSIONS. THIS SHOULD HELP IN QUICKENING THE EDIT/BROWSE PROCESS.
+
+ THE ENTRIES GIVEN ABOVE SHOW HOW TO CORRECTLY ENTER DATASET NAMES.
+ ANY DATASET TO BE BROWSED OR EDITED MUST BE CATALOGED. PRESENTLY
+ THERE IS NO PROVISION TO ENTER THE DASD VOLUME FOR AN UNCATALOGED
+ DATASET. BUT THIS CAN BE EASILY DONE.
+
+
)INIT
)PROC
)END
```

Figure 3.19.   Help panel for extended edit/browse.

```
/**********************  REXX  ***********************/
/* AUTHOR: BARRY K. NIRMAL                           */
/****************************************************/
DO FOREVER
  "ISPEXEC DISPLAY PANEL(XEDTBRO)"
  SAVE = ' '
  IF RC ¬= 0 THEN EXIT
  DSN = VALUE('NDSN'SEQ)
  IF DSN = ' ' THEN
    DO
      SAY 'THE DATASET NAME PASSED TO EXEC XEDTBRO IS NULL.'
      SAY 'PLEASE ENTER THE NAME OF THE DATASET TO BE EDITED/BROWSED:'
      PULL DSN
    END
  X = SYSDSN(DSN)
  IF X \= 'OK' THEN
    SAY 'DATASET OR PDS MEMBER ' DSN ' NOT CATALOGED OR NOT AVAILABLE'
  ELSE
  IF F = 'B' THEN
    DO
      "ISPEXEC BROWSE DATASET("DSN")"
      SAVE = 'DATASET BROWSED'
    END
  ELSE
    DO
      "ISPEXEC EDIT DATASET("DSN")"
      IF RC = 0 THEN
        SAVE = '..... DATASET SAVED  .....'
      ELSE
        SAVE = '..... DATASET NOT SAVED .....'
    END
END
EXIT
```

Figure 3.20.   Exec for extended edit/browse.

enter TSO TIME on the command line to display current time and date.

If you do not copy the help panel of Figure 3.19, it will do little harm. You can still use this facility to browse or edit any dataset. However, when you press the HELP key on the extended edit/browse panel, ISPF will display a panel with the heading ISPF DIALOG ERROR, indicating that panel XHELP was not found. But the extended edit/browse panel is so self-describing that it needs little additional explanation. The help panel is only necessary if this facility is to be used by novice programmers or endusers.

3.11.3.   How Does This Facility Work?

Let us suppose the user enters the following command to invoke the exec of Figure 3.20:

```
TSO %XEDTBRO
```

The system will search the datasets allocated to SYSEXEC for member XEDTBRO and, failing to find it, will search SYSPROC. Suppose the system finds XEDTBRO in a dataset allocated to SYSEXEC. The system will invoke the exec shown in Figure 3.20. On line 4 we start a DO loop that is to be executed repeatedly, that is, almost forever. (Even though the DO instruction has the keyword FOREVER, this loop is not executed forever, because on line 7 when RC is found to be nonzero, the EXIT instruction would terminate the exec.) On line 5, panel XEDTBRO is displayed. The system will search all datasets allocated to ISPPLIB for member XEDTBRO and, finding it, will display it. The panel shown in Figure 3.18 will be displayed. Now the user is presented with a screen that looks like the one shown in Figure 3.18. Nothing happens until the user presses a key.

Let us examine this panel. In the ATTR (attribute) section, we define the characters and the attributes associated with them. For example, we specify that the + character is for text that will be displayed in low intensity, and that the underscore character is to start an input field in which the user can key something that will be displayed in low intensity.

In the BODY section, we describe the main body of the panel. You will find that the following are the only unprotected (i.e., keyable) fields, because only these field names are preceded by an underscore or a dollar character:

Variable Name	Purpose
ZCMD	Command entered on the command line
F	Action field in which the user will enter E to specify edit or B to specify browse
SEQ	Dataset number that is to be edited or browsed
NDSN1	Dataset number 1
NDSN2	Dataset number 2
- - -	
- - -	
NDSN30	Dataset number 30

In the INIT (initialization) section, we specify the actions to be taken prior to displaying the panel. The first line specifies that variable F is to be set to null. (&Z is a system variable that contains null.) The next line specifies that when the panel is displayed, the cursor should be positioned at the field associated with variable F. The last line specifies that when the user presses the HELP key on this panel, panel XHELP should be displayed.

Now let us see what we are specifying in the processing (PROC) section. When the user enters some data on the panel and presses a key such as Enter or PF3, the instructions specified in the processing section are carried out. The first line specifies that variable F must be nonblank, that is, the user must enter something in that field. So if the user does not enter anything in the action field, or enters only blanks, the message ENTER REQUIRED FIELD will be automatically displayed in the top right corner of the screen. The next line specifies that the value of F entered by the user must be in the list E and B. If the user enters, say, A in the action field, the message INVALID

VALUE will be automatically displayed. In the same manner, on the next line we specify the edit rule for variable SEQ. The VPUT command specifies that the named variables should be stored by the system in the profile subpool. This is to ensure that the next time this panel is displayed, the previously saved contents of variables will be displayed on the panel. The PROFILE operand ensures that eventually the variables will be saved in a member of the ISPF profile library that is allocated to DDname ISPPROF.

Now suppose the user enters E in the action field, 1 in the dataset number field, and PDS.DOC in the first dataset name field. When the Enter key is pressed, control flows to line 6 in Figure 3.20, that is, to the line immediately following the line where the panel was displayed. At this point RC is zero. (RC was set by the ISPEXEC DISPLAY command. Remember, in REXX every time a command is issued, RC is set. Thus RC contains the return code from the most recently issued command.)

On line 6 we move a blank to variable SAVE. (Note: SAVE is displayed in the top right corner of the extended edit/browse panel.) On line 7 RC would be found to be zero, and the EXIT instruction would not be executed. On line 8 we use the VALUE function to move the content of variable NDSN1 into variable DSN. (If the user had entered 14 in the SEQ field, DSN would be set to the content of NDSN14.) So, in this example, DSN would assume the value PDS.DOC. On line 15 we use the SYSDSN function to check if the dataset name stored in DSN exists. Suppose dataset 'prefix.PDS.DOC' exists. Control would flow to line 19. Since F has the value E, the DO loop started on line 25 would be executed. On line 26 we would issue the ISPEXEC command to invoke ISPF edit for dataset 'prefix.PDS.DOC'. Now the user is presented with the edit panel.

Suppose the user makes a change to the dataset. When he or she presses the END key on the edit panel, control will flow to line 27 in Figure 3.20. Since the user made some change to the dataset being edited, RC would be zero. Line 28 would be executed, followed by line 31 and then line 32. The END instruction on line 32 signals the end of the DO FOREVER loop started on line 4. Control flows to line 5, where the ISPEXEC command is executed to again display the extended edit/browse panel.

What happens when the user presses the HELP key on the extended edit/browse panel? If the user presses the HELP key or enters HELP on the command line of the extended edit/browse panel, control does not come to the exec of Figure 3.20. Instead, ISPF knows that the HELP key was pressed. (Remember, even when you display the extended edit/browse panel in the exec of Figure 3.20, it is big brother ISPF that is sitting on top, monitoring and controlling everything.) Since ISPF was informed through a line in the initialization section of the panel definition shown in Figure 3.18 that the help panel was XHELP, it searches the datasets allocated to ISPPLIB for member XHELP and, finding it, displays it. On the help panel, when the user presses the END key, ISPF displays the extended edit/browse panel.

What happens when the user presses the END key on the panel of Figure 3.18? If the user presses the END key or enters END on the command line of the extended edit/browse panel, control comes to line 6 in the exec of Figure 3.20, that is, to the line immediately following the line where the ISPEXEC DISPLAY command was issued to display the extended edit/browse panel. RC at this point is 8. The EXIT instruction on line 7 is executed, terminating the execution of this exec. Control flows back to ISPF, because it was ISPF that had invoked this exec as a result of the user issuing command TSO %XEDTBRO. ISPF now displays the panel where command XEDTBRO was issued.

What happens when the user presses the RETURN key on the panel of Figure 3.18? If the user presses the RETURN key or enters RETURN on the command line of the extended edit/browse panel, control comes to line 6 in the exec of Figure 3.20, that is, to the line immediately following the line where the ISPEXEC DISPLAY command was issued to display the extended edit/browse panel. RC at this point is 8. The EXIT instruction on line 7 is executed, terminating the execution of this exec. Control flows back to ISPF, because it was ISPF that had invoked this exec as a result of the user issuing command TSO %XEDTBRO. ISPF knows that the user had pressed the RETURN key; it now displays the ISPF primary menu panel.

What happens when the user enters =3 on the command line of the panel of Figure 3.18? In this case, control flows to line 6 in the exec of Figure 3.20, that is, to the line immediately following the line where the ISPEXEC DISPLAY command was issued to display the extended edit/browse panel. RC at this point is 8. The EXIT instruction on line 7 is executed, terminating the execution of this exec. Control flows back to ISPF, because it was ISPF that had invoked this exec as a result of the user issuing command TSO %XEDTBRO. ISPF knows that the user had entered =3 on the panel; it now displays the ISPF utility menu panel.

To find out if control comes back to the exec, you can insert the following line after line 5 in Figure 3.20:

```
SAY 'RIGHT AFTER THE ISPEXEC DISPLAY COMMAND. RC = ' RC
```

What happens when the user presses the RETURN key on the ISPF browse panel? In this case, control flows to line 22 in the exec of Figure 3.20, that is, to the line immediately following the line where the ISPEXEC BROWSE command was issued to invoke ISPF browse. Then control flows to lines 23 and 32, and then to lines 4 and 5. The ISPEXEC DISPLAY command is executed but panel XEDTBRO is not displayed. Rather, ISPF immediately sends control to line 6, because it knows that previously the RETURN key was pressed. RC at this point is 8. The EXIT instruction on line 7 is executed, terminating the execution of this exec. Control flows back to ISPF, because it was ISPF that had invoked this exec as a result of the user issuing command TSO %XEDTBRO. ISPF knows that the user had pressed the RETURN key; it now displays the ISPF primary menu.

What would happen if you delete line 7 in Figure 3.20? Suppose you entered the XEDTBRO command. The panel of Figure 3.18 would be displayed. On this panel suppose you choose to browse a dataset that is cataloged. When you press the Enter key, control will flow to the exec and the browse panel for the dataset will be displayed. At this point, suppose you press the RETURN key. The system will go into an infinite loop, because there is no longer any EXIT instruction in Figure 3.20 to terminate the exec.

3.12. AN IMPROVED FACILITY FOR EXTENDED EDIT, BROWSE, AND SUBMIT

The facility described in the previous section is very helpful. But when I used it for awhile, I found that when I wanted to edit or browse a particular dataset, I had to look up the panel to find out its sequence number, and enter that number in the sequence field. I thought it would be easier if I could take the cursor to the left of a particular dataset I wanted to edit or browse, and enter E to edit it, or B to browse it. I felt that it would also be very helpful if I could enter S to submit a sequential dataset (or a PDS member) as a batch job, because many times, even though I did not want to modify a dataset but merely submit it, I had to go through the time-consuming process of first selecting the dataset for edit, displaying its contents, issuing the SUBMIT command, and then pressing the END key to get out of edit. So I modified the facility presented in the previous section. The enhanced facility consists of just one panel, shown in Figure 3.21, and one exec, shown in Figure 3.22.

3.12.1. Procedure for Installing This Facility

Step 1. Copy the panel shown in Figure 3.21 in member XPANEL of a partitioned dataset that is usually allocated to DDname ISPPLIB during your TSO session.

Step 2. Copy the REXX exec shown in Figure 3.22 in member XPANEL of a partitioned dataset that contains REXX execs or CLISTs, and that is allocated to DDname SYSEXEC or SYSPROC during your TSO session.

3.12.2. How to Display the Extended Edit/Browse Panel

There are three methods of displaying and using the panel shown in Figure 3.21.

Method 1. From the command line of any ISPF panel, enter the following command:

```
TSO %XPANEL
```

This will display the panel shown in Figure 3.21. On this panel, leave the command line blank, and enter dataset names in one or more of the 30 dataset name fields. To select any of them, move the cursor to the left of the dataset name field, and enter E for edit, B for browse, and S to submit the job in that dataset. S can only be specified if the dataset name you entered is either sequential or a PDS member. (If the dataset is partitioned, you will receive a message saying that member TEMPNAME was not found in that dataset.) On the browse or edit panel thus received, when you press the END key you will receive the panel shown in Figure 3.21. And when you press the END key on the extended edit/browse/submit panel, you will receive the panel where you had entered the XPANEL command.

Method 2. If you enter the REXX exec of Figure 3.21 as a command in your ISPF command table, you can pop in and out of extended edit/browse/submit from any other ISPF panel. Suppose you add it to the command table under name FP; then, on the command line of any ISPF panel, you can simply enter FP to invoke this exec and obtain the panel shown in Figure 3.21. Read Section 6.6 in Chapter 6 to learn how the ISPF command table works and how to add a REXX exec or a CLIST to the ISPF command table.

Method 3. You need to determine the dataset containing your primary ISPF panel. Suppose your TSO prefix is Z1BKN and your primary ISPF panel is in Z1BKN.ISPPLIB(ISR@PRIM). You can modify this panel by inserting option F as follows:

```
%   F + Extended Edit/Browse/Submit Facility
```

(If option F is being used for some other task, you can choose some other letter, e.g., X.) Then, in the lower part of the file where normally there is one line for handling each option, you can insert a line as follows to handle this option:

```
F,'CMD(%XPANEL)'
```

Then when you select option F on your ISPF primary menu, you will receive the extended edit/browse/submit panel, provided this

```
)ATTR
 %  TYPE(TEXT)   INTENS(HIGH)
 +  TYPE(TEXT)   INTENS(LOW) SKIP(ON)
 _  TYPE(INPUT)  INTENS(LOW)    JUST(LEFT) PAD(' ') CAPS(ON)
 &  TYPE(INPUT)  INTENS(HIGH)   JUST(LEFT) PAD(' ') CAPS(ON)
 #  TYPE(OUTPUT) INTENS(HIGH)   JUST(LEFT) PAD(' ') CAPS(OFF)
)BODY
% -- EXTENDED EDIT/BROWSE/SUBMIT BY NIRMAL  ------#SAVE
%COMMAND --->_ZCMD
+
+ ENTER SELECTION CODE: E = EDIT, B = BROWSE, S = SUBMIT THE JOB.
+ THE FIRST SELECTION CODE ENTERED IS THE ONE THAT WILL BE USED.
+
%          DATASET NAME (MAX 44 CHARACTERS)                    DATASET NAME
% <--------------------------------------------->  <----------------------------->+
_A1 $NDSN1                                          _A16$NDSN16                    +
_A2 $NDSN2                                          _A17$NDSN17                    +
_A3 $NDSN3                                          _A18$NDSN18                    +
_A4 $NDSN4                                          _A19$NDSN19                    +
_A5 $NDSN5                                          _A20$NDSN20                    +
_A6 $NDSN6                                          _A21$NDSN21                    +
```

```
_A7 $NDSN7                                        _A22$NDSN22          +
_A8 $NDSN8                                        _A23$NDSN23          +
_A9 $NDSN9                                        _A24$NDSN24          +
_A10$NDSN10                                       _A25$NDSN25          +
_A11$NDSN11                                       _A26$NDSN26          +
_A12$NDSN12                                       _A27$NDSN27          +
_A13$NDSN13                                       _A28$NDSN28          +
_A14$NDSN14                                       _A29$NDSN29          +
_A15$NDSN15                                       _A30$NDSN30          +
+
)INIT
)PROC
  &CMD = TRUNC (&ZCMD,'.')
  VPUT (NDSN1,NDSN2,NDSN3,NDSN4,NDSN5,NDSN6,NDSN7,NDSN8,NDSN9,NDSN10,
        NDSN11,NDSN12,NDSN13,NDSN14,NDSN15,NDSN16,NDSN17,NDSN18,NDSN19,
        NDSN20,NDSN21,NDSN22,NDSN23,NDSN24,NDSN25,NDSN26,NDSN27,NDSN28,
        NDSN29,NDSN30) PROFILE
)END
```

Figure 3.21.   Panel for extended edit/browse/submit.

141

```rexx
   /*********************** REXX ***************************/
 1 /* AUTHOR: BARRY K. NIRMAL                            */
 2 /******************************************************/
 3 DO FOREVER
 4   DO I = 1 TO 30
 5     INTERPRET 'A'I '= "_" '
 6   END
 7   "ISPEXEC DISPLAY PANEL(XPANEL)"
 8   IF RC ¬= 0 THEN EXIT
 9   SAVE = ' '
10   DO I = 1 TO 30
11     ACT = VALUE('A'I)
12     DSN = VALUE('NDSN'I)
13     IF ACT ¬= '' & ACT ¬= '_' THEN
14       CALL MAIN_RTN
15   END
16 END
17 EXIT
18 MAIN_RTN:
19 IF DSN = '' THEN
20   DO
21     SAY 'THE DATASET NAME PASSED TO EXEC XPANEL IS BLANK'
22     SAY 'PLEASE ENTER THE NAME OF THE DATASET TO BE EDITED/BROWSED:'
23     PULL DSN
24   END
```

```
26    X = SYSDSN(DSN)
27    IF X ¬= 'OK' THEN
28       DO
29          SAY 'DATASET OR PDS MEMBER ' DSN ' NOT CATALOGED OR NOT AVAILABLE.'
30          SAY 'NOTE THE FOLLOWING SYSTEM MESSAGE FOR THIS DATASET:'
31          SAY X
32       END
33    ELSE
34       IF ACT = 'B' THEN
35          DO
36             "ISPEXEC BROWSE DATASET(""DSN"")"
37             SAVE = 'DATASET BROWSED'
38          END
39       ELSE
40          IF ACT = 'E' THEN
41             DO
42                "ISPEXEC EDIT DATASET(""DSN"")"
43                IF RC = 0 THEN
44                   SAVE = '.... DATASET SAVED .....'
45                ELSE
46                   SAVE = '.... DATASET NOT SAVED .....'
47             END
48          ELSE
49             IF ACT = 'S' THEN
```

Figure 3.22.   Exec for extended edit/browse/submit.

continues

143

```
50          CALL SUBMIT_RTN
51     ELSE SAVE = 'INVALID SELECTION CODE '
52  RETURN
53  SUBMIT_RTN:
54     " SUBMIT " DSN
55     IF RC = 0 THEN
56        SAVE = 'JOB WAS SUBMITTED'
57     ELSE
58        SAVE = 'ERROR IN JOB SUBMISSION'
59     RETURN
***********************************************************************
```

Figure 3.22. (Continued)

facility has been installed according to the instructions given above.

Once you have obtained the extended edit/browse/submit panel, using it is easy. Figure 3.21 shows the valid options. The main thing to remember is that once you have entered the names of commonly used datasets on this panel, the system will remember them, and the next time you access extended edit/extended browse, the dataset names entered or modified during the last use will be displayed on the panel.

On the panel of Figure 3.21, you can enter any valid TSO command on the command line to execute that command. For example, you can enter TSO TIME on the command line to display current time and date.

3.12.3. Explanation of the Facility

Let us suppose the user enters the following command to invoke the exec of Figure 3.22:

```
TSO %XPANEL
```

The system will search the datasets allocated to SYSEXEC for member XPANEL and, failing to find it, will search SYSPROC. Suppose the system finds XPANEL in a dataset allocated to SYSEXEC. The system will invoke the exec shown in Figure 3.22. On line 4 we start a DO loop that is to be executed repeatedly, that is, almost forever. (Even though the DO instruction has the keyword FOREVER, this loop is not executed forever, because on line 9 when RC is found to be nonzero, the EXIT instruction would terminate the exec.) In the DO loop enclosed between lines 5 and 7, variables A1 through A30 are set to a string consisting of the underscore character followed by two blanks. This is done so that when the panel is displayed, the 30 action code fields will have underscores in them. On line 8, panel XPANEL is displayed. Thus the system will search all datasets allocated to ISPPLIB for member XPANEL and, finding it, will display it. The panel shown in Figure 3.21 will be displayed. Now the user is presented with a screen that looks like the one shown in Figure 3.21. Nothing happens until the user presses a key.

Let us examine this panel. You will find that the following are the only unprotected (i.e., keyable) fields, because only these field names are preceded by an underscore or a dollar character:

Variable Name	Purpose
ZCMD	Command entered on the command line
A1	Action code for dataset number 1
NDSN1	Dataset number 1
A2	Action code for dataset number 2
NDSN2	Dataset number 2
- - -	
- - -	
A30	Action code for dataset number 30
NDSN30	Dataset number 30

Suppose the user enters E in the first action field, and PDS.DOC in the first dataset name field. When the Enter key is pressed, control flows to line 9 in Figure 3.22, that is, to the line immediately following the line where the panel was displayed. At this point RC is zero. (RC was set by the ISPEXEC DISPLAY command.) We will execute the DO loop of line 11. In this loop, when I is 1, variable ACT will be set to the value of A1, that is, E; DSN will be set to PDS.DOC and line 15 will be executed, resulting in internal subroutine MAIN_RTN being called. In this subroutine, we would invoke ISPF edit for dataset 'prefix.PDS.DOC'. In this way you can follow this exec. Note that the general processing in this exec is similar to that described in the previous section.

There are two points worth noting. One is that multiple datasets can be selected for the same or different actions. For example, suppose the user entered B in action code 1 and E in action code 5. First, dataset number 1 will be browsed. When the user presses the END key on the browse panel, he or she will not receive the panel of Figure 3.21, and will immediately receive the edit panel for dataset number 5. When the user presses the END key on the edit panel, he or she will receive the panel shown in Figure 3.21.

The second point concerns the use of the INTERPRET instruction on line 6 and the VALUE function on lines 12 and 13. To understand the VALUE function, suppose A2 contains E, and we are inside the DO loop started on line 11, with I being 2. On line 12, ACT would be set to the content of variable A2, so ACT would be set to E. To fully grasp how the VALUE function works, read the examples under VALUE in Appendix B.

Now let us understand the INTERPRET instruction used on line 6. Suppose the system encounters line 6 and I equals 5. In the first pass, the system will look at the data after the word INTERPRET and build a string after substitution. The string built will be as follows:

```
A5 = "_  "
```

Now this string will be executed as if it was an instruction. This will result in variable A5 being set to a string consisting of the underscore character followed by two blanks. Remember, the INTERPRET instruction and the VALUE built-in function are related. Sometimes VALUE can do what INTERPRET does. In this exec we have used both INTERPRET and VALUE.

3.13   AN EXEC TO DETERMINE IF CURRENT TIME IS WITHIN SPECIFIED LIMITS

In Figure 3.23 is a REXX exec that will receive two parameters representing time limits. It will then decide if the current system time is within these limits. If so, it will end with a return code of zero, otherwise it will end with a return code of 1. If any time value passed to it is not numeric, it will end with a return code of 99. The comments in this figure describe how to invoke this exec from any ISPF panel.

3.13.1.   Use of This Exec in System/Application Design

To understand how this exec can be useful, let us take an example. Suppose you have a job stored in member JOBDLY1 of Z1ABC.JOBS.CNTL. You want this job to be submitted only when the time is within, say, 9.10 a.m. and 10.10 a.m. If the current time

```
*****************************************************************
 1  /***************** REXX *****************************************/
 2  /* THIS EXEC RECEIVES TWO TIME VALUES IN FORMAT HHMM. IF THE CURRENT */
 3  /* SYSTEM TIME IS WITHIN THESE TWO LIMITS, IT EXITS WITH RETURN CODE */
 4  /* OF ZERO, ELSE IT EXITS WITH RETURN CODE OF 1. IF ANY OF THE TWO   */
 5  /* TIME VALUES PASSED TO IT IS NOT NUMERIC, IT EXITS WITH RETURN     */
 6  /* CODE OF 99. FOR EXAMPLE IF THE CURRENT TIME IS 1630 AND YOU ENTER */
 7  /* THE FOLLOWING COMMAND TO INVOKE THIS EXEC:                        */
 8  /*                                                                   */
 9  /*           TSO SETRCT 0910 1600                                    */
10  /*                                                                   */
11  /* IT WILL SET RETURN CODE TO 1, BECAUSE THE CURRENT TIME IS OUTSIDE */
12  /* THE TWO TIME LIMITS SPECIFIED.                                    */
13  /*******************************************************************/
14  /*   TRACE ALL   */
15  ARG TIME1 TIME2 .
16  IF DATATYPE(TIME1) ¬= 'NUM' THEN EXIT 99
17  IF DATATYPE(TIME2) ¬= 'NUM' THEN EXIT 99
18  HOURS   = SUBSTR(TIME(),1,2)
19  MINUTES = SUBSTR(TIME(),4,2)
20  CURR_TIME = HOURS
21  CURR_TIME = INSERT(MINUTES,CURR_TIME,2)
22  IF CURR_TIME < TIME1 THEN EXIT 1
23  IF CURR_TIME > TIME2 THEN EXIT 1
*****************************************************************
```

Figure 3.23.   Exec to determine if specified time is within specified limits.

148

```
*****************************************************************
1  //JOBNAME    JOB STATEMENT GOES HERE
2  //*===========================================================*
3  //* STEP01 WILL END IN CONDITION CODE OF ZERO ONLY WHEN THE CURRENT *
4  //* TIME IS WITHIN THE TWO TIME LIMITS (FORMAT HHMM) SPECIFIED ON THE *
5  //* EXEC STATEMENT. NOTE: MEMBER SETRCT MUST EXIST IN THE PDS THAT IS *
6  //* ALLOCATED TO DDNAME SYSEXEC.                             *
7  //*===========================================================*
8  //STEP01   EXEC PGM=IRXJCL,PARM='SETRCT 0910 1010'
9  //SYSEXEC  DD  DISP=SHR,DSN=Z1ABC.EXEC
10 //SYSTSPRT DD  SYSOUT=*
11 //SYSTSIN  DD  DUMMY
12 //*===========================================================*
13 //* BYPASS THE FOLLOWING STEP IF THE FIRST STEP ENDED IN NON-ZERO *
14 //* CONDITION CODE, I.E. IF THE CURRENT TIME IS NOT WITHIN THE TIME *
15 //* LIMITS SPECIFIED ON THE EXEC STATEMENT IN STEP01.        *
16 //*===========================================================*
17 //STEP02   EXEC PGM=IEBGENER,COND=(0,NE,STEP01)
18 //SYSPRINT DD  SYSOUT=*
19 //SYSUT1   DD  DISP=SHR,DSN=Z1ABC.JOBS.CNTL(JOBDLY1)
20 //SYSUT2   DD  SYSOUT=(A,INTRDR)
21 //SYSIN DD DUMMY
*****************************************************************
```

Figure 3.24.   A job that executes the exec of Figure 3.23.

149

is outside these limits, the job must not be submitted. You cannot depend on a human being for this, because a human is prone to error. He or she may submit this job at the wrong time. So how do you achieve this objective? The job in Figure 3.24 shows you how.

Let us see how it works. You ask an operator or user to submit this job or release it for execution at any time between 9.10 and 10.10 hours. Even if he or she submitted it or released it for execution at the wrong time, it would not submit the actual job. Let us see how. In the first step we execute the exec named SETRCT, which in this example resides in partitioned dataset Z1ABC.EXEC. This exec is shown in Figure 3.23. On line 8 in this job we specify the two time limits. The first step will end in condition code of 0 if the current time is within 9.10 and 10.10 hours; otherwise it will end in condition code of 1. In the second step, we use IEBGENER to submit the job that resides in member JOBDLY1 of Z1ABC.JOBS.CNTL. This is done by writing this file to the MVS internal reader.

The COND parameter, line 17 in this job, specifies that if the condition code of the first step is not zero, the second step should be bypassed. This means that if the current time is not within 9.10 and 10.10 hours, the second step would be bypassed and the job stored in member JOBDLY1 of Z1ABC.JOBS.CNTL would not be submitted. So even if the operator or user submitted the job of Figure 3.24 at the wrong time, it would not submit the actual job.

You can use the exec of Figure 3.23 in any manner you see fit. Basically I have described how you can use it to ensure that a job or job step can be executed or bypassed if the current time is within the two specified time limits. Systems programmers and applications analysts know that if a job is run at the wrong time, it may cause serious problems, such as initializing the contents of system datasets. Thus this facility can be helpful in ensuring that human error in submitting a job at the wrong time, or submitting multiple jobs, does not cause serious problems in systems.

3.14.   AN EXEC TO DETERMINE THE CURRENT DAY OF THE WEEK

You can consult a textbook on mathematics or computer algorithms and find the algorithm to figure out the day of the week for any specified date. For example, suppose we want to know whether January 1, 1917 was a Sunday, a Monday, a Tuesday, and so on; this algorithm will figure it out. You can write a REXX exec that accepts a date or takes the system date as default and figures out the day of the week for that date. It terminates with a return code of 0 for a Sunday, 1 for a Monday, and so on. The technique of setting a return code in a REXX exec and using such an exec in a batch job to control the execution of subsequent job steps was illustrated in the previous section.

3.14.1. Use of This Exec in System/Application Design

This exec can be useful to both systems and applications programmers in a situation like this. Suppose your application or system has many programs. On Sundays you want certain programs to be executed, on Mondays you want some other programs to be executed, and so on. To take a specific example, suppose PROG01 should be run only on Sundays, and PROG02 only on Mondays. Rather than build many jobs and ask the computer operator or a user to submit job 1 on Sunday, job 2 on Monday, and so on, you can build just one job. The first step of this job will execute the exec that figures out the day of the week. The remaining steps will have the COND parameter to control their execution. In this example, since PROG01 should be executed only on Sundays, and the REXX exec returns a condition code of zero for Sunday, and 1 for Monday, you can have the following:

```
//STEP01  EXEC PGM=IRXJCL,PARM='DETDAY'
- - -
- - -
//STEPSUN EXEC PGM=PROG01,COND=(0,NE,STEP01)
- - -
- - -
//STEPMON EXEC PGM=PROG02,COND=(1,NE,STEP01)
- - -
- - -
```

4

Using REXX to Build Some Useful Utilities

In this chapter we discuss how to use REXX execs to build useful utilities. We also present utilities that are ready to install and use. Both applications and systems programmers can immensely benefit from the tools and techniques presented. These tools will make your programming tasks much easier. Section 4.2 presents a complete case study to illustrate the technique of using REXX execs, ISPF panels, and COBOL programs to build online facilities under ISPF. All these programs and routines are highly practical in nature and have proven to be very useful to the author in his day-to-day work as an information systems analyst and consultant.

4.1. A COBOL PROGRAM AND REXX EXEC TO ENCRYPT THE CONTENT OF ANY MEMBER OF A PARTITIONED DATASET

Figure 4.1 shows COBOL program TRANSFOR, and Figure 4.2 shows a REXX exec that can be used to execute this program. These two programs enable us to encrypt/decrypt the content of any sequential dataset, or any member of any PDS that has 80-byte records.

```
ID DIVISION.
PROGRAM-ID. TRANSFOR
AUTHOR.       BARRY K. NIRMAL
ENVIRONMENT DIVISION.
CONFIGURATION SECTION.
INPUT-OUTPUT SECTION.
FILE-CONTROL.
    SELECT SOURCE-FILE ASSIGN TO UT-S-SOURCE.
    SELECT NEW-FILE ASSIGN TO UT-S-NEW.
DATA DIVISION.
FILE SECTION.
FD  SOURCE-FILE
    BLOCK CONTAINS 0
    LABEL RECORDS ARE STANDARD.
01  SOURCE-REC      PIC X(80).
FD  NEW-FILE
    BLOCK CONTAINS 0
    LABEL RECORDS ARE STANDARD.
01  NEW-REC         PIC X(80).
WORKING-STORAGE SECTION.
01  EOF-SW          PIC X VALUE ZERO.
01  COUNTER         PIC 99.
01  A               PIC 99.
01  B               PIC 99.
01  CHAR-SAVE       PIC X.
01  RECORD1.
    10 CHAR1 PIC X OCCURS 80 TIMES.
01  RECORD2.
    10 CHAR2 PIC X OCCURS 80 TIMES.
01  RECORDA.
    10 CHARA PIC X OCCURS 80 TIMES.
01  RECORDB.
    10 CHARB PIC X OCCURS 80 TIMES.
01  RECORDX.
    10 CHARX PIC X OCCURS 80 TIMES.
PROCEDURE DIVISION.
    PERFORM 010-INITIALIZE-PROGRAM THRU 010-EXIT.
    PERFORM 020-READ-TRANSFORM-WRITE THRU 020-EXIT
      UNTIL EOF-SW = '1'.
    PERFORM 030-TERMINATE-PROGRAM THRU 030-EXIT.
    GOBACK.
010-INITIALIZE-PROGRAM.
    OPEN INPUT SOURCE-FILE OUTPUT NEW-FILE.
010-EXIT. EXIT.
020-READ-TRANSFORM-WRITE.
    READ SOURCE-FILE INTO RECORD1 AT END
        MOVE '1' TO EOF-SW
```

Figure 4.1.   Source code of program to encrypt or decrypt the content of any sequential file with 80-byte-long records.

continues

```
        GO TO 020-EXIT.
    READ SOURCE-FILE INTO RECORD2 AT END
        PERFORM ODD-NUMBER THRU ODD-EXIT
    ELSE
        PERFORM EVEN-NUMBER THRU EVEN-EXIT.
020-EXIT.  EXIT.
ODD-NUMBER.
    MOVE 1 TO COUNTER.
    PERFORM 027-MIX-ODD THRU 027-EXIT UNTIL COUNTER > 80.
    MOVE RECORDA TO RECORDX.
    PERFORM 090-MIX-AND-WRITE THRU 090-EXIT.
    MOVE '1' TO EOF-SW.
ODD-EXIT. EXIT.
EVEN-NUMBER.
    MOVE 1 TO COUNTER.
    PERFORM 025-MIX-EVEN THRU 025-EXIT UNTIL COUNTER > 80.
    MOVE RECORDB TO RECORDX.
    PERFORM 090-MIX-AND-WRITE THRU 090-EXIT.
    MOVE RECORDA TO RECORDX.
    PERFORM 090-MIX-AND-WRITE THRU 090-EXIT.
EVEN-EXIT. EXIT.
025-MIX-EVEN.
    MOVE COUNTER TO A.
    COMPUTE B = 81 - COUNTER.
    MOVE CHAR1 (A) TO CHARA (B).
    MOVE CHAR2 (A) TO CHARB (B).
    COMPUTE COUNTER = COUNTER + 1.
025-EXIT.  EXIT.
027-MIX-ODD.
    MOVE COUNTER TO A.
    COMPUTE B = 81 - COUNTER.
    MOVE CHAR1 (A) TO CHARA (B).
    COMPUTE COUNTER = COUNTER + 1.
027-EXIT.  EXIT.
090-MIX-AND-WRITE.
    PERFORM 091-MIX THRU 091-EXIT VARYING COUNTER FROM
      1 BY 2 UNTIL COUNTER > 80.
    WRITE NEW-REC FROM RECORDX.
090-EXIT.  EXIT.
091-MIX.
    COMPUTE A = COUNTER + 1.
    MOVE CHARX (COUNTER) TO CHAR-SAVE.
    MOVE CHARX (A) TO CHARX (COUNTER).
    MOVE CHAR-SAVE TO CHARX (A).
091-EXIT.  EXIT.
030-TERMINATE-PROGRAM.
    CLOSE SOURCE-FILE NEW-FILE.
030-EXIT.  EXIT.
```

Figure 4.1.   (Continued)

```
*************************************************************
1  /******************** REXX *********************************/
2  /* Author: Barry K. Nirmal                                 */
3  /***********************************************************/
4  /* If the input member name is say ABC, the output member name will be*/
5  /* ABCT. After that if you transform member ABC, this EXEC will read */
6  /* member ABCT and write records in member ABC. So, if the last char. */
7  /* of an input member you specify is not T, the member name must not */
8  /* be more than 7 characters. This is becouse this EXEC will append */
9  /* T to the member name to determine the output member name. */
10 /***********************************************************/
11 /* The user can enter zzzz or ZZZZ when prompted for PDS member name, */
12 /* if he wants to terminate this EXEC. Because of automatic upper-case*/
13 /* translation, the program will find ZZZZ in memin after the Pull */
14 /* instruction has executed. */
15 /***********************************************************/
16 Say 'This command allows you to transform one or more members'
17 Say 'of a PDS that must have 80-byte long records.'
18 pds = ''
19 Do while pds = ''
20   Say 'Enter the name of the PDS (fully-qualified but no quotes please):'
21   Pull pds
22 End
23 done = 'no'
24 Do while done = 'no'
25   memin = ''
26   Do while memin = ''
27     Say 'Enter the name of PDS member to be transformed (zzzz to End) =>'
28     Pull memin
29   End
30   If memin = 'ZZZZ' Then done = 'yes'
```

```
31   Else NOP
32   If done = 'no' Then do
33      len1 = length(memin)
34      len2 = len1 - 1
35      lastchar = substr(memin,len1,1)
36      memout = memin
37      if lastchar = 'T' Then
38         memout = substr(memin,1,len2)
39      Else
40         memout = Insert('T',memout,len1,1)
41      If length(memout) > 8 Then Do
42         Say 'Output Member Name is Longer than 8 Characters.'
43         Say 'EXEC TRANSFOR is being abnormally terminated.'
44         Say 'Correct This Error; then Rerun This EXEC Please.'
45         Exit
46      End
47      Say 'The name of the input PDS    member is =====>' memin
48      Say 'The name of the transformed member will be ===>' memout
49      "Free F(Source New Sysdbout Sysudump)"
50      "Alloc f(source) da('"pds"("memin")') Shr"
51      "Alloc f(new)    da('"pds"("memout")') Shr"
52      "Alloc f(sysdbout) da(*)"
53      "Alloc f(sysudump) sysout(Q) "
54      "Call  'userid.loadlib(transfor)' "
55   End
56   End
57   "Free f(source new sysdbout sysudump)"
58   exit 0
```

****

Figure 4.2. A REXX exec to execute the program of Figure 4.1.

157

4.1.1. How Can This Facility Be Useful to IS Professionals?

Suppose you have created a confidential memo or a special program in a member of your PDS. Naturally, you don't want anyone to be able to browse this file. You have many choices to protect your dataset. First, you can ask the software security group at your installation to protect your PDS so that only you can browse it. But the problem is that there are users (e.g., TSO IDs) who have special attributes (called noncancelable in ACF/2) that enable them to access any dataset. The manager of the security or systems programming group is also normally able to browse any dataset. So this method will not protect your dataset from those users.

Another method is to protect your dataset with an OS password by issuing this TSO command from option 6 of ISPF:

```
PROTECT dataset-name ADD(pwd) PWREAD
```

(where suitable values must be supplied for dataset-name and pwd because they are in lower case).

This command will protect your dataset so that only those people who know its password can browse or update it. But the problem again is that systems programmers have tools that enable them to find the OS password of any dataset. You are not protected from them.

The best method is to use the facility given here. But before using it you might want to modify the encryption logic contained in program TRANSFOR shown in Figure 4.1. This is because this book may be in the hands of another person in your company, who will be able to use this program to decrypt your file. Once you have changed this program, only you know the new encryption logic used. You may also want to give the program a new name, so that only you know its name. Now test that the new program is able to encrypt and decrypt any source file successfully. After that, print the new program and take it home. Delete its source from your system. Take care that only you know the name of the load module and how to use it. Now you are protected from everyone.

4.1.2.   Procedure for Installing This Facility

Step 1. Copy the content of Figure 4.1 into member TRANSFOR of a source PDS.

Step 2. Copy the content of Figure 4.2 into member ENCR of a PDS that contains all your REXX execs. See Section 1.9 in Chapter 1 to find out how to create a PDS that contains REXX execs.

Step 3. Compile and link program TRANSFOR using a JCL deck that you normally use to compile and link a batch COBOL program. This job will create load module TRANSFOR in your load library.

Step 4. Modify exec ENCR as follows. On line 54 replace userid.loadlib with the full name of your load library in which you linked program TRANSFOR in Step 3 above. On line 53 you may want to assign sysout to a class other than Q. The class you will use should be valid at your installation, and it should be assigned to the TSO held output class. The installation of this facility is now complete.

   Note: Suppose you use TRANSFOR to encrypt file A and create file B. When you use TRANSFOR to transform file B, you will get back file A. This is to say that the encryption logic used in TRANSFOR is such that when the same logic is used to transform the transformed file, the original file is obtained. I call such encryption logic "symmetrical."

4.1.3.   Procedure for Using This Facility

Suppose you have a PDS named Z1ABC.PDS80 in which exists member SPCLDOC. You want to encrypt this member. If the exec of Figure 4.2 is stored as member ENCR in a library that is allocated under DDname SYSEXEC or SYSPROC during your TSO session, you may execute it by entering the following on the command line of any ISPF panel:

```
TSO %ENCR
```

This exec will prompt you for the PDS name. You will enter the following:

```
z1abc.pds80
```

Next it will prompt you for the member name. You will enter the following:

```
spcldoc
```

The exec will figure out the name of the output PDS member. It will inform you that the name of the input PDS member will be SPCLDOC and that of the output PDS member will be SPCLDOCT. (See how it appends T to the name of the input member to arrive at the name of the output member. If the input member name already had T at the end, the exec would assume that its content is encrypted, so it would remove the T from the input name to arrive at the output member name.) It will then call program TRANSFOR to carry out the encryption, which would write encrypted records into member SPCLDOCT. Then the exec will prompt you for another PDS member name to be encrypted or decrypted. If you want to stop here, enter zzzz or ZZZZ as the member name. This will terminate the exec.

Now your encrypted file is in member SPCLDOCT. For security reasons, you may now delete member SPCLDOC. Suppose three months later, you wanted to decrypt your file. You would again run exec ENCR. This time you would enter SPCLDOCT as input member name. The exec will tell you that the output member name will be SPCLDOC. It will then call program TRANSFOR, which will read member SPCLDOCT and write decrypted records into member SPCLDOC.

4.1.4.   Explanation of REXX Exec ENCR

When you execute this exec, execution starts from the first line of the exec. Lines 1 through 15 in this exec are comments. On lines 16 and 17 we display messages on the screen, telling the user what this exec does. (This is very important from the standpoint of making online facilities user-friendly.) On line 18 we assign null as the value of variable pds. On lines 19 through 22 we prompt the user for PDS name. If the user simply pressed the Enter key, the value of pds stored as a result of the Pull instruction on line 21 would be null. This would cause lines 20 and 21 to be executed again. Only when the user types something and presses the Enter key will the control flow to line 23.

On line 24 we start a DO WHILE loop that has its end on line 56. Because done is 'no', we execute line 25. The code on lines 25 through 29 is used to prompt the user for the PDS member name and store it in variable memin. Only when the user enters a value on the terminal and presses the Enter key would control flow to line 30. On line 30 we check if the member name entered by the user is zzzz or ZZZZ. If so, we set done to 'yes'. On line 32 we test if the value of done equals 'no'. If so, we start a DO loop that is bounded by lines 33 and 55. Suppose the user entered SPCLDOC for memin. In this case, control would flow to line 33. On subsequent lines we figure out the name of the output member and store it in variable memout. The value of memout in this example would be SPCLDOCT.

On line 41 we check if the length of memout exceeds 8. If so, we would display messages on lines 42, 43, and 44 and terminate execution on line 45. In this example, the length of memout is 8, so control would flow to line 47. On lines 47 and 48 we would display the names of input and output members on the terminal. On line 49 we would free up some DDnames. On line 50 we allocate the input PDS member under DDname SOURCE, and on line 51 we allocate the output PDS member under DDname NEW. On line 52 DDname SYSDBOUT is allocated to the terminal, and on line 53 DDname SYSUDUMP is allocated to sysout class Q. On line 54 the CALL command of TSO is used to execute program TRANSFOR, whose source code is given in Figure 4.1. Control then flows to line 55 and then to line 56. Since line 56 marks the ending for the DO WHILE of line 24, execution of line 56 sends control back to line 24, where a check is made if done equals 'no'. In this example, it would be true, so line 25 would be executed and the processing described above would again take place. Only when the user enters zzzz or ZZZZ when prompted for the PDS member name would control flow to line 57, where we would free up a number of DDnames. Next, the exit instruction on line 58 would terminate the execution of the exec.

4.1.5. Explanation of Program TRANSFOR

This program follows the two-level transformation described below in transforming the input file into the output file. Suppose the input file has records designated as r1, r2, r3, . . . , rn. The output file will have the records which can be designated as R1, R2, R3, R4, R5, R6, . . . , Rn. In the first-level transformation, R1 is derived from r2, R2 from r1, R3 from r4, R4 from r3, and so on. The method of deriving output record from input record is by:

- Interchanging the characters at positions 1 and 80.
- Interchanging the characters at positions 2 and 79.
- Interchanging the characters at positions 3 and 78.
- - -
- - -
- Interchanging the characters at positions 39 and 42.
- Interchanging the characters at positions 40 and 41.

This way all records are transformed. You can see that each input record is modified, and in each pair of modified input records the second modified input record is written first, followed by the first output record. If the input record has an odd number of records, the last modified input record is written out as the last output record. (Even though we have talked here about "writing" of output records, no records are written to the physical file until after the second transformation. This "writing" can be thought of as occurring in an imaginary holding file.)

Once the above transformation has taken place, each output record is transformed again, in the following manner.

- Characters at positions 1 and 2 are interchanged.
- Characters at positions 3 and 4 are interchanged.
- - -
- - -
- Characters at positions 79 and 80 are interchanged.

Now the transformed records are written out to the output file allocated under DDname NEW. You can follow through the logic in the program of Figure 4.1 and verify that the two-level transformation described above is indeed carried out.

4.2. CASE STUDY OF DEVELOPING AN ONLINE SYSTEM USING ISPF PANELS, REXX EXECS, AND COBOL PROGRAMS

Let us take a practical case study to illustrate the technique of developing user-friendly, online facilities using ISPF panels, REXX execs, and COBOL programs. The components of this system are shown in Figures 4.3 through 4.7 (below). The best method for learning to use the facilities provided by this system is to install it according to the instructions given below, and then to use each facility according to the instructions for using it.

First let us see how to install this facility. We will then discuss using it.

4.2.1. Procedure for Installing This Facility

Here is the procedure to install this facility, leaving aside the VSAM reorganization component, that is, option 3 of Figure 4.3.

Step 1. Copy the panel shown in Figure 4.3 in member BKNUTIL of a partitioned dataset that is usually allocated to DDname ISPPLIB during your TSO session. To explain this point, suppose your TSO prefix is Z1BKN and during your TSO session, DDname ISPPLIB is allocated to many datasets, one of which is Z1BKN.ISPPLIB. To find out the datasets allocated to ISPPLIB, issue this command from the command line of any ISPF panel:

```
TSO LISTA ST H
```

This will show you not only ISPPLIB but all the other DDnames that are currently allocated.

In member BKNUTIL of Z1BKN.ISPPLIB, you can copy the content of Figure 4.3.

Step 2. Copy the REXX execs shown in Figures 4.4 through 4.7 in a partitioned dataset that contains REXX execs or CLISTs, and that is allocated to DDname SYSEXEC or SYSPROC during your TSO session. Again, to find out the datasets allocated to SYSEXEC or SYSPROC, issue this command from the command line of any ISPF panel:

```
*****************************************************************
 1  %-------------------------------------------------------------
 2  %SELECT OPTION ===>_OPT      % Programmer's Tool Box by Barry Nirmal
 3  %
 4  %  0+DELETE ONE OR MORE DATA SETS (VSAM OR NON-VSAM)
 5  %  1+DISPLAY INFO ABOUT ONE OR MORE DATA SET NAMES (FULL)
 6  %  2+DISPLAY INFO ABOUT ONE OR MORE DATA SET NAMES (PARTIAL)
 7  %  3+SUBMIT ONE JOB TO REORGANIZE ONE VSAM KSDS
 8  %  4+Edit %Telephone  + File
 9  %  6+
10  %  7+
11  %  8+
12  %  8+
13  %  9+
14  %  A+
15  %  B+
16  %  C+
17  %  D+
18  %  E+
```

```
19 %    F+                   %X+EXIT FROM SCREEN
20 %
21 %
22 % +PRESS%RETURN+KEY TO EXIT FROM THIS SCREEN
23 +
24 )INIT
25 )PROC
26    &SEL = TRANS( TRUNC (&OPT,'.')
27                  0,'CMD(%DSDEL)'
28                  1,'CMD(%DSINFO)'
29                  2,'CMD(%DSLEVEL)'
30                  3,'CMD(%VSAMORG)'
31                  4,'CMD(%EDTPHONE)'
32                  ' ',' '
33                  X,'EXIT'
34                  *,'?' )
35 )END
```

****

Figure 4.3.   The Programmer's Tool Box panel.

165

```
    /********************* REXX *********************/
 1  /*                                              */
 2  /* Author: Barry K. Nirmal                      */
 3  /************************************************/
 4  /* Reads a sequential file containing list of data set names. For each*/
 5  /* data set, it issues the TSO DELETE command. Make sure that in the  */
 6  /* file this exec reads, every non-comment line has spaces in columns */
 7  /* 45 through 133. Any line with an asterisk in column 1 is treated   */
 8  /* as a comment and ignored.                    */
 9  /************************************************/
10  status = MSG('off')
11  "ispexec Edit dataset(parmlib(dsdel))"
12  "Alloc f(dsnames) da(parmlib(dsdel)) shr reuse"
13  dsncount = 0
14  done = 'no'
15  do while done = 'no'
16    "execio 1 diskr dsnames "
17    if RC = 0 then
18    do
19      pull record
20      if substr(record,1,1) ¬= '*'   Then
```

```
21      do
22          dsncount = dsncount + 1
23          stripline = STRIP(record,t)
24          "Delete '"stripline"'"
25          if RC = 0 then Say stripline ' has been deleted'
26          else DO
27              say stripline ' was not deleted. Probably it does not '
28              say 'Exist, or it is allocated to another user.'
29              say 'Find out why it was not deleted. Thanks a lot.'
30              End
31      end
32      else nop
33      End
34      Else done = 'yes'
35  end
36  "execio 0 diskr dsnames (FINIS" /* Close so file can be freed */
37  "Free f(dsnames outfile)"
38  Say 'Sir/Madam, Number of data sets processed: ' dsncount
39  exit 0
```

****

Figure 4.4.   REXX exec DSDEL for option 0 of the panel of Figure 4.3.

```
 1  /********************* REXX *********************/
 2  /* Author: Barry K. Nirmal                      */
 3  /************************************************/
 4  /* Reads a sequential file containing list of data set names. For each*/
 5  /* data set, it will issue LISTCAT, WHOHAS and other commands.        */
 6  /* Make sure a line with data set name has spaces in positions        */
 7  /* 45 through 133. Any line with an asterisk in position 1 is treated */
 8  /* as a comment and ignored.                                          */
 9  /************************************************/
10  status = MSG('OFF')
11  "ispexec Edit dataset(parmlib(dsinfo))"
12  "Free da(listc.print) "
13  "Delete Listc.Print"
14  "Free f(dsnames OUTFILE) "
15  "Alloc f(OUTFILE) da(listc.print) MOD dsorg(ps) tracks space(10 10)
16       lrecl(125) blksize(629)  recfm(V B A)"
17  "Alloc f(dsnames) da(parmlib(dsinfo)) shr reuse"
18  dsncount = 0
19  done = 'no'
20  do while done = 'no'
21    "execio 1 diskr dsnames "
22    if RC = 0 then
23      do
```

```
24    pull record
25    if substr(record,1,1) ¬= '*'       Then
26    do
27       dsncount = dsncount + 1
28       stripline = STRIP(record,t)
29       "whohas '"stripline"'"
30       "LISTC ent('"stripline"') all ofile(outfile)"
31       Rcode = RC      /* Save Return Code from LISTCAT */
32       If RCODE ¬= 0 Then
33          Say stripline ' Not Present in Catalog. ** ERROR ** ERROR '
34       Else
35          Say stripline ' Present in Catalog. '
36       end
37    else nop
38    End
39    Else done = 'yes'
40 end
41 "execio 0 diskr dsnames (FINIS" /* Close so file can be freed */
42 "Free f(dsnames outfile) "
43 Say 'Sir/Madam, Number of data sets processed: ' dsncount
44 "ispexec browse dataset(listc.print)"
45 exit 0
****************************************************************************
```

Figure 4.5.   REXX exec DSINFO for option 1 on the panel of Figure 4.3.

169

```
   /*************************** REXX *********************************/
 1 /* Author: Barry K. Nirmal                                      */
 2 /****************************************************************/
 3 /* Reads a sequential file containing list of data set names (partial)*/
 4 /* For each, it will issue  LISTCAT LEVEL command.               */
 5 /* Make sure a line with data set name has spaces in positions   */
 6 /* 45 through 133. Any line with an asterisk in position 1 is treated */
 7 /* as a comment and ignored.                                     */
 8 /****************************************************************/
10 status = MSG('OFF')
11 "ispexec Edit dataset(parmlib(dslevel))"
12 "Free da(listc.print) "
13 "Delete Listc.Print"
14 "Free f(dsnames OUTFILE) "
15 "Alloc f(OUTFILE) da(listc.print) MOD dsorg(ps) tracks space(10 10)
16         lrecl(125) blksize(629)  recfm(V B A)"
17 "Alloc f(dsnames) da(parmlib(dslevel)) shr reuse"
18 dsncount = 0
19 done = 'no'
20 do while done = 'no'
21    "execio 1 diskr dsnames "
22    if RC = 0 then
23       do
24          pull record
```

```
25   if substr(record,1,1) ¬= '*'  Then
26      do
27         dsncount = dsncount + 1
28         stripline = STRIP(record,t)
29         "LISTC Level("stripline") all ofile(outfile)"
30         Rcode = RC    /* Save Return Code from LISTCAT */
31         If RCODE ¬= 0  Then
32            Say stripline ' Not Present in Catalog as level  ** ERROR '
33         Else
34            Say stripline ' Present in Catalog as level'
35      end
36   else nop
37   End
38   Else done = 'yes'
39 end
40 "execio 0 diskr dsnames (FINIS" /* Close so file can be freed */
41 "Free f(dsnames outfile) "
42 Say 'Sir/Madam, Number of file names (partial) processed: ' dsncount
43 "ispexec browse dataset(listc.print)"
44 exit 0
```
****

Figure 4.6.   REXX exec DSLEVEL for option 2 on the panel of Figure 4.3.

171

```
****************************************************************************/
    1  /****************** REXX *****************************************/
    2  /* Author: Barry K. Nirmal                                    */
    3  /*************************************************************/
    4  "ispexec Edit dataset(docpds($phone))"
    5  exit 0
****************************************************************************
```

Figure 4.7.   REXX exec EDTPHONE for option 4 on the panel of Figure 4.3.

172

```
TSO LISTA ST H
```

This will show you not only SYSEXEC but all the other DDnames that are currently allocated. Suppose you find that Z1BKN.EXEC is allocated to DDname SYSEXEC, and that Z1BKN.CLIST is allocated to DDname SYSPROC. You can copy Figure 4.4 in member DSDEL of Z1BKN.EXEC or Z1BKN.CLIST, copy Figure 4.5 into member DSINFO in the same PDS, copy Figure 4.6 in member DSLEVEL, and copy Figure 4.7 in member EDTPHONE of the same PDS.

Step 3. In this step you will modify the execs to suit your environment. The execs that you copied use the following partitioned datasets:

'prefix.DOCPDS'

Member $PHONE of this PDS is supposed to contain the names and telephone numbers of your friends and business contacts.

'prefix.PARMLIB'

In member DSDEL of this PDS you are supposed to enter the names of datasets that you want deleted; in member DSINFO the names of datasets about which you need information; and in member DSLEVEL the first or the first few qualifiers of the names of datasets about which you need information. Other members of this PDS may contain any other data you choose.

So you have two choices. Either you can allocate the above two datasets as partitioned datasets (using ISPF 3.2 or in a batch job using IEFBR14) with logical record length of 80, or you can change the execs copied in step 2 above to use your own datasets. Suppose you choose the latter course. If your TSO prefix is GEN09 and you want to use dataset GEN09.PDS.DATA, you have to do the following:

* In Figure 4.4 change parmlib on lines 11 and 12 to PDS.DATA
* In Figure 4.5 change parmlib on lines 11 and 17 to PDS.DATA
* In Figure 4.6 change parmlib on lines 11 and 17 to PDS.DATA
* In Figure 4.7 change docpds on line 4 to PDS.DATA

Step 4. In Figure 4.5 on line 29, the WHOHAS command is used
to display which users are currently allocated a dataset. At your
installation, this command may be known by another name. If so,
change whohas on line 29 to that name. If your installation does
not have a command that works like whohas, you may delete line
29 from Figure 4.5 and still keep this exec useful and functional.

4.2.2. How to Display the Programmer's Tool Box Panel

The first task is to display the panel shown in Figure 4.3. This
can be done using one of two methods.

Method 1. Assuming that this panel has been copied in member
BKNUTIL of a PDS that is allocated to DDname ISPPLIB during
your TSO session, you can go to native TSO (not TSO within
ISPF) and issue this command:

```
ISPSTART PANEL(BKNUTIL)
```

This will display the panel shown in Figure 4.3. On this panel
when you enter X as an option and press the Enter key, or when
you press the key (normally PF3 or PF15) assigned to the END
command, you will be taken to the native TSO mode, because
this is where you issued the ISPSTART command to display the
Programmer's Tool Box panel.

Method 2. This method, which is better than Method 1, requires
you to determine the dataset containing your primary ISPF panel.
Suppose your TSO prefix is Z1BKN and your primary ISPF panel
is in Z1BKN.ISPPLIB(ISR@PRIM). You can modify this panel by
inserting an option, for example, option P as follows:

```
%  P  +Programmer's Tool Box
```

Then in the lower part of the file where normally there is one line
for handling each option, you can insert a line as follows to handle
option P:

```
P,'PANEL(BKNUTIL)'
```

Then when you select option P from your ISPF primary menu, you will receive the Programmer's Tool Box panel, provided this panel has been copied in member BKNUTIL of a PDS that is allocated to DDname ISPPLIB during your TSO session.

4.2.3.   How to Use This Facility to Delete Datasets

First display the Programmer's Tool Box panel as described above. Type 0 in the option field and press Enter. The system will display the edit panel for editing member DSDEL of your PDS (the default PDS is 'prefix.parmlib' unless changed during installation). Here you can enter the fully qualified names of datasets that you want deleted, starting in column 1. So if you wanted to delete datasets 'SYS2.TEMPLIB' and 'SYS3.LINKLIB', you would enter the following two lines:

```
SYS2.TEMPLIB
SYS3.LINKLIB
```

If you want to delete n datasets, you will enter n records in this dataset. Any record that has an asterisk in column 1 will be ignored. This allows you to insert comments. When you are finished, press the key assigned to the END command (normally PF3 or PF15).

The system will issue a DELETE command against each dataset name that you entered in member DSDEL. A message will be displayed indicating whether the dataset was successfully deleted. At the end, the system will display the count of the number of datasets against which DELETE commands were issued.

How does this facility work? When you enter option 0 on the Programmer's Tool Box panel, the system invokes exec DSDEL, shown in Figure 4.4. What makes the system do so? On line 27 in Figure 4.3 we specify that when the user enters option 0, the system is to invoke command %DSDEL. Because this command starts with the percent sign, the system first searches the datasets allocated to DDname SYSEXEC for member DSDEL. If it is found, it will be executed; otherwise the system will search the datasets allocated to SYSPROC. (This is fully explained in Section 1.10.3 in Chapter 1.) Since during installation we had copied the exec of Figure 4.4 in member DSDEL of a library allocated to SYSEXEC or SYSPROC, the system invokes it.

Control flows to line 10 in Figure 4.4. On line 11 we execute the ISPEXEC command to invoke ISPF Edit for member DSDEL of PDS parmlib. The user is presented with the edit panel, where he or she can add, delete, or change lines, the same way any other dataset is edited using ISPF Edit. When the user presses the key assigned to the END command (normally PF3 or PF15), control flows to line 12 in Figure 4.4. Here we allocate DDname DSNAMES to member DSDEL of PARMLIB. In the logic that follows, we read each line from this dataset. (The EXECIO on line 16 fetches one record from the file.) On line 20 we check if the first character of the record is an asterisk. If so, it is bypassed; otherwise on line 23 we strip the trailing blanks from the record and store the resulting string in variable STRIPLINE, which now contains a dataset name only. On line 24 we issue the DELETE command against the dataset name stored in STRIPLINE. On line 25 we check if the return code returned from the DELETE command is zero. If so, on line 25 we display a message saying that the dataset has been deleted; otherwise on lines 26 through 30 we display a number of lines saying that the dataset was not deleted. When all records in the input file allocated to DDname DSNAMES have been read and processed, control flows to line 36, where we close that DDname. This allows us to free that DDname. On line 37 we free up two DDnames. On line 38 we display a message indicating the total number of datasets against which DELETE commands were issued. When the EXIT instruction on line 39 is executed, the execution of this exec terminates and control flows to ISPF, which displays the Programmer's Tool Box panel, because it was from this panel that we had invoked exec DSDEL.

4.2.4.   How to Use This Facility to Display Information About One or More Datasets with Fully Qualified Names

First display the Programmer's Tool Box panel as described above. Type 1 in the option field and press Enter. The system will display the edit panel for editing member DSINFO of your PDS (the default

PDS is 'prefix.parmlib' unless changed during installation). Here you can enter the fully qualified names of datasets about which you want information, starting in column 1. If you wanted information about datasets 'SYS2.PROCLIB' and 'SYS3.LINKLIB', you would enter the following two lines:

```
SYS2.PROCLIB
SYS3.LINKLIB
```

If you wanted information about n datasets, you would enter n records in this dataset. Any record that has an asterisk in column 1 will be ignored. This allows you to inserts comments. When you are finished, press the key assigned to the END command (normally PF3 or PF15).

For each dataset you entered in member DSINFO, the system will first issue the WHOHAS command to display the users who might be using that dataset. Then it will issue the LISTC command to display information from the MVS catalog for that dataset. The output of the LISTC command will be appended at the end of sequential file 'prefix.LISTC.PRINT' where prefix is your TSO prefix. (This file is deleted and then allocated in this exec. See lines 13 and 15–16 of Fig. 4.4.) The system will also display on the terminal a message indicating whether the dataset for which it issued the LISTC command is present in the catalog. After processing all records from member DSINFO, the system will display the count of the number of datasets against which WHOHAS and LISTC commands were issued. Next the system will display the ISPF browse panel for dataset 'prefix.LISTC.PRINT', which contains output from the LISTC commands issued for all the datasets. You can browse this dataset just as you browse any other dataset using ISPF Browse. When you press the key assigned to the END command (normally PF3 or PF15), you will receive the Programmer's Tool Box panel.

How does this facility work? When you enter option 1 on the Programmer's Tool Box panel, the system invokes exec DSINFO, shown in Figure 4.5. What makes the system do so? On line 28 in Figure 4.3 we specify that when the user enters option 1, the system is to invoke command %DSINFO. Because this command starts with the percent sign, the system first searches the datasets allocated to DDname SYSEXEC for member DSINFO. If it is found, it will be executed; otherwise the system will search the datasets allocated to SYSPROC. (This is fully explained in Section 1.10.3 in Chapter 1.) Since during installation we had copied the exec of Figure 4.5 in member DSINFO of a library allocated to SYSEXEC or SYSPROC, the system invokes it.

Control flows to line 10 in Figure 4.5. On line 11 we execute the ISPEXEC command to invoke ISPF Edit for member DSINFO of PDS parmlib. The user is presented with the edit panel, where he or she can add, delete, or change lines, the same way any other dataset is edited using ISPF Edit. When the user presses the key assigned to the END command (normally PF3 or PF15), control flows to line 12 in Figure 4.5. Here we free up dataset 'prefix.LISTC.PRINT', where prefix is user's TSO prefix. On line 13 we delete this dataset, and on the next line we allocate it again. This is done to get rid of any old records that might be present in the dataset. On line 17 we allocate DDname DSNAMES to member DSINFO of PARMLIB. In the logic that follows, we read each line from this dataset. (The execio on line 21 fetches one record from the file.) On line 25 we check if the first character of the record is an asterisk. If so, it is bypassed; otherwise on line 28 we strip the trailing blanks from the record and store the resulting string in variable STRIPLINE, which now contains dataset name only. On line 29 we issue the WHOHAS command against the dataset name stored in STRIPLINE. This will display the users who might be using that dataset. On line 30 we issue the LISTC command with the ENTRY option against the dataset name stored in STRIPLINE. The OFILE option on the LISTC command indicates that the messages from the command are to be written to DDname OUTFILE. Since OUTFILE was allocated on line 15 with disposition of MOD, the LISTC messages will get appended to the end of the file allocated to OUTFILE.

On line 32 we check if the return code returned from the LISTC command is nonzero. If so, on line 33 we display a message saying that the dataset is not present in the catalog; otherwise on line 35 we display a message saying that the dataset is present in the catalog. When all records in the input file allocated to DDname DSNAMES have been read and processed, control flows to line 41, where we close that DDname. This allows us to free that DDname. On line 42 we free up two DDnames. On line 43 we display a message indicating the total number of datasets against which WHOHAS and LISTC commands were issued.

On line 44 we issue the ISPEXEC command to display the browse panel for dataset 'prefix.LISTC.PRINT'. The user can now browse that dataset. When he presses the key assigned to the END command, control flows to line 45 in Figure 4.5. Here the EXIT instruction is executed, which terminates the execution of this exec. Control now flows to ISPF, which displays the Programmer's Tool Box panel, because it was from this panel that we had invoked exec DSINFO.

4.2.5.   How to Use This Facility to Display Information About Datasets with Specified Prefixes

First display the Programmer's Tool Box panel as described above. Type 2 in the option field and press Enter. The system will display the edit panel for editing member DSLEVEL of your PDS (the default PDS is 'prefix.parmlib' unless changed during installation). Here you can enter the first or the first few (but not all) qualifiers of the names of datasets about which you want information, starting in column 1. If you wanted information about datasets that start with PRCAS and those that start with SYS2.PROD, you would enter the following two lines:

```
PRCAS
SYS2.PROD
```

Any record that has an asterisk in column 1 will be ignored. This allows you to insert comments. When you are finished, press the key assigned to the END command (normally PF3 or PF15).

For each dataset level you entered in member DSLEVEL, the system will issue the LISTC command with LEVEL option to display information for that dataset level from the MVS catalog. The output of the LISTC command will be appended at the end of sequential file 'prefix.LISTC.PRINT' where prefix is your TSO prefix. The system will also display on the terminal a message indicating whether that dataset level is present in the catalog. After processing all records from member DSLEVEL, the system will display the count of the number of dataset levels against which LISTC commands were issued. Next the system will display the ISPF browse panel for dataset 'prefix.LISTC.PRINT', which contains output from all the LISTC commands issued. You can browse this dataset just as you browse any other dataset using ISPF Browse. When you press the key assigned to the END command (normally PF3 or PF15), you will receive the Programmer's Tool Box panel.

How does this facility work? When you enter option 2 on the Programmer's Tool Box panel, the system invokes exec DSLEVEL shown in Figure 4.6. What makes the system do so? On line 29 in Figure 4.3 we specify that when the user enters option 2, the system is to invoke command %DSLEVEL. Because this command starts with the percent sign, the system first searches the datasets allocated to DDname SYSEXEC for member DSLEVEL. If it is found, it will be executed; otherwise the system will search the datasets allocated to SYSPROC. (This is fully explained in Section 1.10.3 in Chapter 1.) Since during installation we had copied the exec of Figure 4.6 in member DSLEVEL of a library allocated to SYSEXEC or SYSPROC, the system invokes it.

So control flows to line 10 in Figure 4.6. On line 11 we execute the ISPEXEC command to invoke ISPF Edit for member DSLEVEL of PDS parmlib. The user is presented with the edit panel, where he or she can add, delete, or change lines, the same way any other dataset is edited using ISPF Edit. When the user presses the key assigned to the END command (normally PF3 or PF15), control flows to line 12 in Figure 4.6. Here we free up dataset 'prefix.LISTC.PRINT', where prefix is user's TSO prefix. On line 13 we delete this dataset, and on the next line we allocate it again. This is done to get rid of any old records that might be present in the dataset. On line 17 we allocate DDname DSNAMES to member DSLEVEL of PARMLIB. In the logic that follows, we read each line from this dataset. (The execio on line 21 fetches one record from the file.) On line 25 we check if the first character of the record is an asterisk. If so, it is bypassed; otherwise on line 28 we strip the trailing blanks from the record and store the resulting string in variable STRIPLINE, which now contains the dataset name only. On line 29 we issue the LISTC command with the LEVEL option against the dataset name stored in STRIPLINE. The OFILE option on the LISTC command indicates that the messages from the command are to be written to DDname OUTFILE. Since OUTFILE was allocated on line 15 with disposition of MOD, the LISTC messages will get appended to the end of the file allocated to OUTFILE.

On line 31 we check if the return code returned from the LISTC command is nonzero. If so, on line 32 we display a message saying that the dataset level is not present in the catalog; otherwise on line 34 we display a message saying that the dataset level is present in the catalog. When all records in the input file allocated to DDname DSNAMES have been read and processed, control flows to line 40, where we close that DDname. This allows us to free that DDname. On line 41 we free up two DDnames. On line 42 we display a message indicating the total number of dataset levels against which LISTC commands were issued.

On line 43 we issue the ISPEXEC command to display the browse panel for dataset 'prefix.LISTC.PRINT'. The user can now browse that dataset. When he presses the key assigned to the END command, control flows to line 44 in Figure 4.6. Here the EXIT instruction is executed, which terminates the execution of this exec. Control now flows to ISPF, which displays the Programmer's Tool Box panel, because it was from this panel that we had invoked exec DSLEVEL.

4.2.6. How to Use This Facility to Display and Maintain Information in the Telephone Dataset

First display the Programmer's Tool Box panel as described above. Type 4 in the option field and press Enter. The system will display the edit panel for editing member $PHONE of your PDS (the default PDS is 'prefix.DOCPDS' unless changed during installation). This dataset is supposed to contain names and telephone numbers of your friends and business contacts. You can browse the data present in the telephone dataset and/or change it. Remember, you are editing this dataset; you can use the same commands that you use when editing any dataset using ISPF Edit. When you are finished, press the key assigned to the END command (normally PF3 or PF15). You will receive the Programmer's Tool Box panel.

How does this facility work? When you enter option 4 on the Programmer's Tool Box panel, the system invokes exec EDTPHONE, shown in Figure 4.7. What makes the system do so? On line 31 in Figure 4.3 we specify that when the user enters option 4, the system is to invoke command %EDTPHONE. Because this command starts with the percent sign, the system first searches the datasets allocated to DDname SYSEXEC for member EDTPHONE. If it is found, it will be executed; otherwise the system will search the datasets allocated to SYSPROC. (This is fully explained in Section 1.10.3 in Chapter 1.) Since during installation we had copied the exec of Figure 4.7 in member EDTPHONE of a library allocated to SYSEXEC or SYSPROC, the system invokes it.

Control flows to line 4 in Figure 4.7. On this line we execute the ISPEXEC command to invoke ISPF Edit for member $PHONE of PDS docpds. The user is presented with the edit panel, where he or she can add, delete, or change lines, the same way any other dataset is edited using ISPF Edit. When the user presses the key assigned to the END command (normally PF3 or PF15), control flows to line 5 in Figure 4.7. Here the EXIT instruction is executed, which terminates the execution of this exec. Control now flows to ISPF, which displays the Programmer's Tool Box panel, because it was from this panel that we had invoked exec EDTPHONE.

Some REXX Execs Especially Useful for Systems Programmers

In this chapter we present a number of REXX execs that will be of special interest to the systems programmers who support or work with MVS. The execs presented will demonstrate the power and versatility of the REXX language. They will also demonstrate the ability of even a small REXX program to easily fetch the content of any location within the address space and to quickly navigate through the control blocks, jumping from one control block to another, in search of the desired piece of information. This sort of ability and power fills the hearts of systems programmers with joy.

5.1.   AN EXEC TO DEFINE AN ALIAS IN THE MASTER CATALOG

Suppose an applications programmer wants to allocate a dataset with prefix PAYROLL. Before he or she can do so, this prefix must be defined as an alias in the MVS master catalog. That is, an alias-type entry must exist in the master catalog specifying the name of the user catalog that is to contain all the datasets with that prefix. In our example, suppose that user catalog ICAT.CICS10 is to contain all the datasets with prefix PAYROLL. An alias-type entry must be created in the master catalog that specifies that user catalog ICAT.CICS10 will contain all the datasets with prefix PAYROLL. To define this alias, you can issue the following TSO command:

```
DEFINE ALIAS(NAME(PAYROLL) RELATE('ICAT.CICS10'))
```

But rather than burden yourself with having to remember the exact syntax of this command, you can write a REXX exec that will automate this task. Such an exec will also make it easy for even nontechnical or less-technical staff to perform this task. Such an exec is shown in Figure 5.1. If this exec is stored in member DEFALI of a PDS that is allocated to DDname SYSEXEC or SYSPROC during the user's TSO session, he or she can execute it by entering the following on the command line of any ISPF panel:

```
TSO %DEFALI
```

It will prompt the user for the name of the alias (i.e., prefix) to be defined and the name of the user catalog to which this alias is to be related. Then it will issue the DEFINE ALIAS command. This command will prompt the user for the password of the master catalog, because the master catalog, being a highly important resource, is usually password-protected so that only those who know its password can update it. If the password entered is correct and the alias was successfully defined, the following message will be displayed:

```
ALIAS alias HAS BEEN SUCCESSFULLY DEFINED.
```

5.1.1. How to Display All the Aliases Defined in the Master Catalog

From TSO within ISPF (option 6) or native mode TSO (READY mode), issue this command to set your prefix to null:

```
PROFILE NOPREFIX
```

Now issue the following command to display the names of all the aliases present in the master catalog:

```
*****************************************************************************
1    /****************** REXX ******************************************/
2    /* EXEC: DEFALI      Author: Barry K. Nirmal                    */
3    /****************************************************************/
4    /* trace all    */
5    Say 'You will be prompted for information. At any time, you may press'
6    Say 'the PA1 key to cause premature termination of this command. Thanks'
7    say '_____.'
8    prefix = ''
9    usercat = ''
10   Do while prefix = ''
11     Say 'Kindly Enter the Prefix to be Defined (No Quotes):'
12     Pull prefix
13   End
14   do while usercat = ''
15     Say 'Kindly Enter the Full Name of the User Catalog (No Quotes):'
16     Pull usercat
17   End
18   say 'Note the following please:'
19   say 'The Prefix to be Defined is : ' prefix
20   say 'User Catalog to Which This Prefix Will be Related is: ' usercat
21   say '_____.'
22   "DEFINE ALIAS(NAME('"prefix"') RELATE('"usercat"'))"
23   If RC = 0 Then
24     Say 'ALIAS ' prefix ' HAS BEEN SUCCESSFULLY DEFINED.'
25   Else Say 'Error occurred while executing the DEFINE ALIAS command'
26   Exit
*****************************************************************************
```

Figure 5.1. An exec to define an alias in the master catalog.

185

```
LISTC ALIAS
```

After this command has finished, you may want to reset your prefix by issuing this command:

```
PROFILE PREFIX(prefix)
```

where you must replace prefix with your actual TSO prefix, which usually, but not necessarily, is identical with your TSO ID.

5.1.2. How to Display the Names of All the User Catalogs

From TSO within ISPF (option 6) or native mode TSO (READY mode), issue this command to set your prefix to null:

```
PROFILE NOPREFIX
```

Now issue one of the following commands to display the names of all the user catalogs present in the master catalog:

```
LISTC USERCAT
LISTC UCAT
```

After this command has finished, you may want to reset your prefix as described in Subsection 5.1.1.

5.1.3. How to Display the Name of the Master Catalog and the User Catalog Name for an Alias

From TSO within ISPF (option 6) or native mode TSO (READY mode), issue this command:

```
LISTC ENT('prefix') ALIAS ALL
```

where you must replace prefix with a valid prefix, for example, your TSO prefix, which usually, but not necessarily, is identical with your TSO ID. The output from this command will look like this:

```
ALIAS — prefix
IN-CAT — name.of.master.catalog
HISTORY
   RELEASE ———2
ASSOCIATIONS
   USERCAT — user.catalog.name
```

This output tells you the name of the master catalog. It also tells you the name of the user catalog associated with the alias (prefix). For example, suppose you issue this command:

```
LISTC ENT('Z1BKN') ALIAS ALL
```

and obtain the following response:

```
ALIAS — Z1BKN
IN-CAT — ICAT.MASTER
HISTORY
   RELEASE ———2
ASSOCIATIONS
   USERCAT — ICAT.CICS10A
```

This tells you that the name of the master catalog is ICAT.MASTER, and the user catalog that contains entries for all datasets and objects with Z1BKN as their prefix is ICAT.CICS10A.

5.2. AN EXEC TO DELETE AN ALIAS FROM THE MASTER CATALOG

Now suppose that alias PAYROLL is to be deleted from the master catalog. The reason is either that this prefix is no longer needed due to the dataset-naming standards of the installation, or that this alias was related to the wrong user catalog when it was defined. What are the steps involved in deleting this alias? The first thing is to issue the following command to check if any datasets with that prefix exist:

```
TSO LISTC L(PAYROLL)
```

If there are any datasets, they would be listed and the return code from this command will be zero. If there are no datasets, a message indicating this will be displayed and the return code will be nonzero.

If there are any datasets with prefix PAYROLL, first they must be either deleted or renamed to assume some other prefix. Then you can issue the following TSO command to delete that alias from the master catalog:

```
DELETE 'PAYROLL' ALIAS CATALOG('ICAT.MASTCAT'/BERRIE)
```

where, in this example, PAYROLL is the alias being deleted, ICAT.MASTCAT is the name of the master catalog, and BERRIE is its update password. You can change PAYROLL to the alias you want deleted, specify the master catalog name and its password so that they are valid for your installation, and then issue this command.

But rather than burden yourself with having to remember the exact syntax of this command, you can write a REXX exec that will automate this task. Such an exec will also make it easy for even nontechnical or less-technical staff to perform this task. Such an exec is shown in Figure 5.2. If this exec is stored in member DELALI of a PDS that is allocated to DDname SYSEXEC or SYSPROC during the user's TSO session, he or she can execute it by entering the following on the command line of any ISPF panel:

```
TSO %DELALI
```

It will prompt the user for the name of the alias (i.e., prefix) to be deleted and the password of the master catalog. (The name of the master catalog need not be entered by the user, because this name does not change frequently. When the master catalog is renamed, the systems programmer can also update this exec.) This exec will then ensure that there are no datasets with the specified prefix before issuing the DELETE ALIAS command. If the password entered is correct and the alias was successfully deleted, the following message will be displayed:

```
ALIAS alias HAS BEEN SUCCESSFULLY REMOVED.
```

5.3.   AN EXEC TO DISPLAY THE NAMES OF LINK-LIST LIBRARIES

Figure 5.3 shows a REXX exec that will display the names of all the link-list libraries defined to the MVS system. As given in the comments in this figure, this exec will display SYS1.LINKLIB as being in the link-list even though this library is not present in member LNKLSTxx of SYS1.PARMLIB. Now the following question arises.

What is link-list? In member LNKLSTxx of SYS1.PARMLIB, the systems programmer specifies the names of load libraries that are to be included in the link-list. At system IPL (initial program load) time, the system reads this member of SYS1.PARMLIB and builds the link-list table in storage. During system execution, this table in storage will be searched rather than member LNKLSTxx of SYS1.PARMLIB. Now let us explain when and why this table is searched.

Suppose in your batch job you execute program A. The following is the order of search under MVS/XA:

- Job Pack Area
- Tasklib (applicable only to user subtasks)
- Steplib/Joblib
- Link Pack Area (MLPA and FLPA are searched before PLPA)
- SYS1.LINKLIB and the Link-List Libraries

Suppose that this program, not being a system program, is not present in system areas such as job pack area, link pack area, and so forth. Your job has no JOBLIB statement but has a STEPLIB statement. The system first searches the STEPLIB library for program A. If it is found, it is executed from there. If it is not found, the system searches SYS1.LINKLIB, and then the other link-list libraries. If program A is found in any library included in the link-list, it is executed from there. If it is not found in any of the link-list libraries, the job step is abnormally ended (abended) with system abend code 806.

How does this exec work? This exec is self-explanatory because we are using meaningful, long variable names. On line

```rexx
  /********************* REXX ****************************/
1 /* EXEC: DELALI       Author: Barry K. Nirmal        */
  /*****************************************************/
2 /* Make sure the name of your master catalog is correctly entered on */
3 /* the DELETE command below. So, you must replace ICAT.MASTCAT with  */
4 /* the full name of your master catalog.             */
5 /*****************************************************/
6
7
8 Say 'You will be prompted for information. At any time, you may press'
9 Say 'the PA1 key to cause premature termination of this cimmand. Thanks'
10 say ' .'
11 prefix = ' '
12 update_pwd = ' '
13 Do while prefix = ' '
14   Say 'Kindly Enter the Prefix to be Deleted (No Quotes):'
15   Pull prefix
16 End
17 do while update_pwd = ' '
18   Say 'Kindly Enter the Update Password for the Master Catalog'
19   Pull udate_pwd
20 End
21 "listc l(""prefix"")"
```

```
22  if rc = 0 Then
23      Do
24          say 'There are still datasets with prefix ' Prefix ' as listed'
25          say 'above. Please delete or rename these datasets before trying'
26          say 'to delete this prefix itself. Thanks for your patience.'
27          exit
28      end
29  /* trace all */
30  "DELETE '"prefix"' ALIAS CATALOG('ICAT.MASTCAT'/"update_pwd")"
31  If RC = 0 Then
32      Say 'ALIAS ' prefix ' HAS BEEN SUCCESSFULLY REMOVED.'
33  Else
34      do
35          Say 'Error occurred while deleting prefix ' prefix
36          Say 'Perhaps this prefix is not defined in the system, or '
37          Say 'the name or the password of the master catalog used on the '
38          Say 'DELETE ALIAS command is not correct. Pls. investigate.'
39      End
40  Exit
```

****

Figure 5.2.   An exec to delete an alias from the master catalog.

```
   /********************************* REXX *************************************/
 1 /* EXEC NAME: SHOWLLT        AUTHOR: BARRY K. NIRMAL                  */
 2 /* THIS EXEC WILL DISPLAY THE DATASET NAME OF EACH LIBRARY IN THE     */
 3 /* LINKLIST TABLE PRESENT IN THE MVS SYSTEM AT THE TIME OF EXECUTION. */
 4 /* THIS EXEC WILL DISPLAY SYS1.LINKLIB AS BEING IN THE LINKLIST TABLE,*/
 5 /* EVEN THOUGH IN THE LNKLSTXX MEMBER OF SYS1.PARMLIB, THIS LIBRARY    */
 6 /* IS NOT PRESENT.                                                    */
 7 /*********************************************************************/
 8 /* BY UNCOMMENTING THE TRACE INSTRUCTION, YOU CAN SEE INTERMEDIATE    */
 9 /* RESULTS. THIS WILL HELP YOU IN UNDERSTANDING THE MVS INTERNALS.    */
10 /*********************************************************************/
11
12 /* TRACE INT    */
13 CVT_ADDR_CHAR                   = STORAGE(10,4)
14 CVT_ADDR_HEX                    = C2X(CVT_ADDR_CHAR)
15 CVT_ADDR_DEC                    = C2D(CVT_ADDR_CHAR)
16 PTR_LINKLIST_TABLE_ADDR_DEC     = CVT_ADDR_DEC + 1244
17 PTR_LINLIST_TABLE_ADDR_CHAR     = D2C(PTR_LINKLIST_TABLE_ADDR_DEC,4)
18 PTR_LINKLIST_TABLE_ADDR_HEX     = C2X(PTR_LINKLIST_TABLE_ACDR_CHAR)
19 LINKLIST_TABLE_ADDR_CHAR        = STORAGE(PTR_LINKLIST_TABLE_ADDR_HEX,4)
```

```
20  LINKLIST_TABLE_ADDR_HEX            = C2X(LINKLIST_TABLE_ADDR_CHAR)
21  A                                  = STORAGE(LINKLIST_TABLE_ADDR_HEX,8)
22  NUMBER_OF_ENTRIES_CHAR             = SUBSTR(A,5,4)
23  NUMBER_OF_ENTRIES_DEC              = C2D(NUMBER_OF_ENTRIES_CHAR)
24  SAY 'NUMBER OF LINKLIST LIBRARIES  = ' NUMBER_OF_ENTRIES_DEC
25  SAY ' '
26  SAY 'THE FOLLOWING ARE THE LINKLIST LIBRARIES DEFINED TO THE SYSTEM'
27  SAY '_____'
28  MAX_LENGTH_POSSIBLE                = (NUMBER_OF_ENTRIES_DEC * 45) + 8
29  LINKLIST_TABLE_DATA = ,
30          STORAGE(LINKLIST_TABLE_ADDR_HEX,MAX_LENGTH_POSSIBLE)
31  START_POSITION = 10
32  DO I = 1 TO NUMBER_OF_ENTRIES_DEC
33    DATASET_NAME = ,
34        SUBSTR(LINKLIST_TABLE_DATA,START_POSTION,44)
35    START_POSITION = START_POSITION + 45
36    SAY DATASET_NAME
37  END
```

****

Figure 5.3.   An exec to display all libraries in the link-list table.

```
  *************************************************************
1 /************************* REXX ******************************/
2 /* EXEC NAME: SHOWAPF    AUTHOR:   BARRY K. NIRMAL          */
3 /* THIS EXEC WILL DISPLAY THE VOLUME SERIAL AND DATASET NAME OF */
4 /* EACH APF LIBRARY DEFINED TO THE MVS SYSTEM.             */
5 /* BY UNCOMMENTING THE TRACE INSTRUCTION, YOU CAN SEE INTERMEDIATE */
6 /* RESULTS. THIS WILL HELP YOU IN UNDERSTANDING THE MVS INTERNALS. */
7 /*************************************************************/
8 /* TRACE INT    */
9 CVT_ADDR_CHAR            = STORAGE(10,4)
10 CVT_ADDR_HEX            = C2X(CVT_ADDR_CHAR)
11 CVT_ADDR_DEC            = C2D(CVT_ADDR_CHAR)
12 PTR_AUTH_TABLE_ADDR_DEC = CVT_ADDR_DEC + 484
13 PTR_AUTH_TABLE_ADDR_CHAR = D2C(PTR_AUTH_TABLE_ADDR_DEC,4)
14 PTR_AUTH_TABLE_ADDR_HEX = C2X(PTR_AUTH_TABLE_ADDR_CHAR)
15 AUTH_TABLE_ADDR_CHAR    = STORAGE(PTR_AUTH_TABLE_ADDR_HEX,4)
16 AUTH_TABLE_ADDR_HEX     = C2X(AUTH_TABLE_ADDR_CHAR)
17 NUMBER_OF_ENTRIES_CHAR  = STORAGE(AUTH_TABLE_ADDR_HEX,2)
18 NUMBER_OF_ENTRIES_DEC   = C2D(NUMBER_OF_ENTRIES_CHAR)
19 SAY 'NUMBER OF APF LIBRARIES IN THE SYSTEM =' NUMBER_OF_ENTRIES_DEC
```

```
20  SAY ' '
21  SAY 'THE FOLLOWING ARE THE APF LIBRARIES DEFINED TO THE SYSTEM'
22  SAY ' '
23  MAX_LENGTH_POSSIBLE      = (NUMBER_OF_ENTRIES_DEC * 51) + 2
24  APF_TABLE_DATA      = STORAGE(AUTH_TABLE_ADDR_HEX,MAX_LENGTH_POSSIBLE)
25  START_POSITION = 3
26  SAY 'VOL-SER    THE NAME OF THE APF LIBRARY'
27  SAY '=======    ====================================='
28  DO I = 1 TO NUMBER_OF_ENTRIES_DEC
29     ENTRY_LENGTH_CHAR = SUBSTR(APF_TABLE_DATA,START_POSITION,1)
30     ENTRY_LENGTH_DEC = C2D(ENTRY_LENGTH_CHAR)
31     LENGTH_OF_DSN = ENTRY_LENGTH_DEC - 6
32     VOLSER = SUBSTR(APF_TABLE_DATA,START_POSITION+1,6)
33     DATASET_NAME = SUBSTR(APF_TABLE_DATA,START_POSITION+7,LENGTH_OF_DSN)
34     START_POSITION = START_POSITION + 1 + ENTRY_LENGTH_DEC
35     SAY VOLSER '    ' DATASET_NAME
36  END
```

****

Figure 5.4.   An exec to display the volumes and names of all the authorized libraries.

13 we obtain the content of 4 bytes at storage location with address Hex'10' (decimal 16). This is the address of the CVT (Communication Vector Table). This address is stored in variable CVT_ADDR_CHAR. On line 14 we convert this address into hexadecimal format, and on line 15 we convert it into decimal format. In the CVT at offset 1244 (decimal) or 4DC (hexadecimal) is the address of the link-list table. On line 19 we fetch the content of 4 bytes at (Address-of-CVT-in-decimal + 1244) and store it in variable LINKLIST_TABLE_ADDR_CHAR. This variable now contains the address of the link-list table in character format. On line 21 we go to the link-list table address, fetch the contents of 8 bytes there, and store it in variable A. Bytes 5 through 8 of A contains the number of entries in the link-list table. On line 23 we store the number of entries in decimal in variable NUMBER_OF_ENTRIES_DEC and on line 24 we display this value.

In the code that follows, we scan the link-list table and display the name of each entry in it.

5.4. AN EXEC TO DISPLAY THE NAMES OF APF LIBRARIES

In Figure 5.4 is a REXX exec that will display the names of all the load libraries that are defined as authorized in the MVS system. This exec will display SYS1.LINKLIB and SYS1.SVCLIB on the system residence (SYSRES) pack as being authorized, even though they are not present in member IEAAPFxx of SYS1.PARMLIB. Now the following question arises.

What is meant by a load library being authorized? In member IEAAPFxx of SYS1.PARMLIB, the systems programmer specifies the names of load libraries that are to be considered authorized. At system IPL (initial program load) time, the system reads this member of SYS1.PARMLIB and builds the APF table in storage. During system execution, this table in storage is searched rather than member IEAAPFxx of SYS1.PARMLIB. A program that uses authorized functions such as MODESET macro to place itself in the supervisor state must run authorized. The best way to make a program authorized is to store it in a load library that is included in the APF list.

How does this exec work? This exec is self-explanatory because we are using meaningful, long variable names. On line 9 we obtain the content of 4 bytes at storage location with address Hex'10' (decimal 16). This is the address of the CVT (Communication Vector Table). This address is stored in variable CVT_ADDR_CHAR. On line 10 we convert this address into hexadecimal format, and on line 11 we convert it into decimal format. In the CVT at offset 484 (decimal) or 1E4 (hexadecimal) is the address of the authorized library (APF) table. On line 15 we fetch the content of 4 bytes at (Address-of-CVT-in-decimal + 484) and store it in variable AUTH_TABLE_ADDR_CHAR. This variable now contains the address of the authorized library table in character format. On line 17 we go to the authorized library table address, fetch the contents of 2 bytes there, and store it in variable NUMBER_OF_ENTRIES_CHAR. This variable now contains the number of entries in the authorized library table in character format. On line 18 we convert this value into the decimal format and on line 19 we display it. In the code that follows, we scan the authorized library table and display the volume and the dataset name of each authorized library in the table.

6

Advanced REXX Programming Techniques

In this chapter we present some advanced REXX programming techniques. These techniques are presented using the question-and-answer format. A number of examples illustrate the programming techniques, because, as it is said, a picture is worth a thousand words.

6.1. SHOW ME THE TECHNIQUE OF WRITING AND USING ISPF EDIT MACROS

Let us illustrate this technique through the examples of four useful edit macros. They are given in Figures 6.1 through 6.4. To install them, you must do the following:

> Copy the content of Figure 6.1 in member BLNKSPCL of a PDS that is allocated to DDname SYSEXEC or SYSPROC during your TSO session. Copy the content of Figure 6.2 in member RECOVON. Copy the content of Figure 6.3 in member RECOVOFF. Copy the content of Figure 6.4 in member TELLCHG of the same PDS.

Edit macros are written as REXX execs or CLISTs, but they mainly contain the ISREDIT commands of ISPF. To learn more about them, consult this IBM publication (or its equivalent, ap-

```
********************************************************************
1  /************** REXX ***********************************/
2  /* THIS EDIT MACRO WILL CHANGE ALL SPECIAL CHARACTERS TO BLANKS.  */
3  /* AUTHOR: BARRY KUMAR NIRMAL                                     */
4  /****************************************************************/
5  "ISREDIT MACRO"
6  "ISREDIT CHANGE ALL P'.' ' ' "
7  "ISREDIT (CHANGES,ERRORS) = CHANGE_COUNTS "
8  "ISREDIT RESET "
9  ZEDLMSG = 'CHANGES= '
10 ZEDLMSG = INSERT(CHANGES,ZEDLMSG,9)
11 ZEDLMSG = INSERT(' ERRORS= ',ZEDLMSG,17)
12 ZEDLMSG = INSERT(ERRORS,ZEDLMSG,26)
13 "ISPEXEC  SETMSG MSG(ISRZ000) "
14 EXIT
********************************************************************
```

Figure 6.1.   An edit macro to change all special characters to blanks.

```
****************************************************************************
 1  /***************** REXX ********************************************/
 2  /* THIS EDIT MACRO WILL TURN ON THE RECOVERY OPTION IN THE EDIT   */
 3  /* PROFILE. THIS WILL ALLOW YOU TO RECOVER CHANGES MADE TO A DATASET */
 4  /* BUT NOT SAVED, IN THE EVENT OF POWER FAILURE OF A SYSTEM CRASH.  */
 5  /* AUTHOR: BARRY KUMAR NIRMAL                                       */
 6  /*****************************************************************/
 7  "ISREDIT MACRO"
 8  ZEDSMSG = 'RECOVERY TURNED ON'
 9  "ISPEXEC SETMSG MSG(ISRZ001)"
10  "ISREDIT RECOVERY ON "
11  EXIT
****************************************************************************
```

Figure 6.2.   An edit macro to turn recovery on.

201

```
  ******************************************************
1 /***************** REXX *****************************/
2 /* THIS EDIT MACRO WILL TURN OFF THE RECOVERY OPTION IN THE EDIT     */
3 /* PROFILE. THIS WILL HOPEFULLY GIVE YOU FASTER RESPONSE. BUT NOTE:  */
4 /* YOU WILL NOT BE ABLE TO RECOVER THE CHANGES MADE TO A DATASET BUT */
5 /* NOT SAVED, IN THE EVENT OF POWER FAILURE OR A SYSTEM CRASH.       */
6 /* AUTHOR: BARRY KUMAR NIRMAL                                        */
7 /***************************************************/
8 "ISREDIT MACRO"
9 ZEDSMSG = 'RECOVERY TURNED OFF'
10 "ISPEXEC SETMSG MSG(ISRZ001)"
11 "ISREDIT RECOVERY OFF"
12 EXIT
  ******************************************************
```

Figure 6.3.   An edit macro to turn recovery off.

```
**************************************************************************
1   /************** REXX **************************************/
2   /* THIS EDIT MACRO WILL TELL YOU IF THE FILE BEING CURRENTLY EDITED */
3   /* HAS BEEN MODIFIED. THIS WILL ASSIST YOU IN DECIDING WHETHER TO   */
4   /* CANCEL OR SAVE THE CHANGES.                                      */
5   /* AUTHOR: BARRY KUMAR NIRMAL                                       */
6   /******************************************************************/
7   "ISREDIT MACRO"
8   "ISPEXEC CONTROL ERRORS RETURN "
9   "ISREDIT (CHANGED) = DATA_CHANGED "
10  IF CHANGED = 'YES' THEN
11      DO
12          ZEDSMSG =  'FILE CHANGED'
13          ZEDLMSG =  'FILE HAS BEEN CHANGED IN THIS SESSION'
14      END
15  ELSE
16      DO
17          ZEDSMSG =  'FILE NOT CHANGED'
18          ZEDLMSG =  'FILE HAS NOT BEEN CHANGED IN THIS SESSION'
19      END
20  "ISPEXEC SETMSG MSG(ISRZ001) "
21  EXIT
**************************************************************************
```

Figure 6.4.   An edit macro to tell you if the file being edited has been changed.

203

plicable to your environment): *ISPF/PDF Version 3 Release 2 MVS Edit and Edit Macros* (SC-34-4253).

Now let us examine our "gang of four" useful edit macros.

6.1.1. An Edit Macro to Change All Special Characters to Blanks

Suppose you are editing a dataset using ISPF Edit and you want to change all the special characters to blanks. To do this in the usual way, you have to first issue the HEX ON command, locate the special characters, and then, one by one, change them to X'40', the hexadecimal representation in EBCDIC of space. But if the edit macro shown in Figure 6.1 has been installed as described above, all you need to do is type BLNKSPCL on the command line of the edit panel and press Enter. The system will invoke this edit macro, which will change all the special characters to spaces. On the line below the COMMAND line, it will also display the number of changes made and errors encountered, for example,

```
CHANGES= 00000005 ERRORS= 00000000
```

This edit macro also illustrates how to write and use edit macros. In it we are using just one ISREDIT CHANGE command. But, if necessary, you may use more than one such command. (Note: If you enter the name of an edit macro, for example, BLNKSPCL, on the command line of any panel other than ISPF Edit, you will receive the message INVALID COMMAND, because it is not a valid ISPF command.)

Technique of quickening the use of an edit macro. Suppose you use an edit macro named EMAC very frequently. Using ISPF option 0, you can assign a PF key to this command so that when you press that PF key, this macro will be invoked. For example, you may decide to assign PF21 to EMAC. So when you are editing a dataset, all you need do is press PF21 and edit macro EMAC will be executed. (Note: On the PF Keys panel of ISPF option 0, you should enter the name of the edit macro after the PF key that you wish to assign to it.)

6.1.2.   An Edit Macro to Set RECOVERY ON

Figure 6.2 shows an edit macro that will turn on the recovery option for the dataset being edited. To use it, just enter RECOVON on the command line of the edit panel when you are editing a dataset. The effect will the same as if you entered RECOVERY ON. But its main benefit is that you can use it as an initial macro at the edit (option 2) panel itself so that any datasets you are editing will automatically have RECOVERY ON in their profile. This will mean that you will be able to recover the changes in case of system crash or an abnormal end (abend).

To consider using this macro for automatically turning recovery on, consider the execs of Figures 3.20 and 3.22 in Chapter 3. These execs support the extended edit/browse facility. In each of these figures, the ISPEXEC EDIT command is used to invoke ISPF edit. If the edit macro of Figure 6.2 has been copied in member RECOVON in a PDS allocated to DDname SYSEXEC or SYSPROC, you can change the following line in Figures 3.20 and 3.22,

```
"ISPEXEC EDIT DATASET("DSN")"
```

to the following:

```
"ISPEXEC EDIT DATASET("DSN") MACRO(RECOVON)"
```

This will have the following effect. Whenever you select a dataset on the extended edit/browse panel for edit, after the records are read but before they are displayed, macro RECOVON will be invoked. It will set RECOVERY ON in the profile, and when you receive the edit panel, the message RECOVERY TURNED ON will appear in the top right corner of the screen.

6.1.3.   An Edit Macro to Set RECOVERY OFF

Figure 6.3 shows edit macro RECOVOFF that turns recovery off. Its use is similar to that of RECOVON described above. I use RECOVOFF in the exec that supports my extended edit/browse panel, because it gives me faster response on my terminal.

6.1.4. An Edit Macro to Display if a File Has Been Modified During the Current Edit Session

Suppose you are editing a dataset using the ISPF editor. You want to know if you have made some change to it since the last time it was saved, or, if it was not saved, since the beginning of edit. This will help you decide if you should cancel the changes or save them. To know this, type TELLCHG on the command line and press the Enter key. If the file has been changed you will receive FILE CHANGED on the top right corner of the screen; otherwise message FILE NOT CHANGED will be displayed. At this point, if you press the HELP key (normally PF1), you will receive one of the following messages on the line just below the COMMAND line:

```
FILE HAS BEEN CHANGED IN THIS SESSION
FILE HAS NOT BEEN CHANGED IN THIS SESSION
```

At this point you can continue editing as usual. When you enter TELLCHG, the REXX exec shown in Figure 6.4 is executed. This exec is actually an edit macro, because the first noncomment line has the ISREDIT MACRO command. Remember, all commands in a REXX exec are enclosed within double quotation marks.

6.2. SHOW ME THE TECHNIQUE OF EXECUTING TSO COMMANDS, CLISTs, AND REXX EXECS IN TSO/E BACKGROUND

Figure 6.5 shows a JCL that can be used to execute any TSO command, a CLIST, or a REXX exec in TSO/E background. (Any TSO command, CLIST, or REXX exec that can be issued from TSO or ISPF can be issued in exactly the same way from TSO/E background.) You will note that we are executing program IKJEFT01. In this example, we are issuing the LISTDS command with the MEM option to list the names of all members present in partitioned dataset 'SYS2.PROCLIB'. After this job has run, dataset Z1BKN.SDSF.PRINT will contain the output from the LISTDS command. This dataset should be allocated as follows:

```
//jobname  JOB Statement
//STEP01   EXEC PGM=IKJEFT01
//SYSTSPRT DD DISP=SHR,DSN=Z1BKN.SDSF.PRINT
//*SYSTSPRT DD SYSOUT=*
//SYSTSIN  DD *
 LISTDS 'SYS2.PROCLIB' MEM
```

Figure 6.5.   A job that executes TSO command LISTDS in TSO/E background.

Record Format: FBA (fixed blocked with carriage control character in column 1 of each record)
Logical Record Length: 133
Block Size: 13300 or any value that is a multiple of 133

Once the job has written records in Z1BKN.SDSF.PRINT, this dataset can be copied into a fixed-blocked dataset with 80-byte records, using ISPF option 3.3. This fixed-blocked dataset can then be manipulated by a program, if so desired.

How can this technique be useful to IS professionals? Let us show some examples.

Example 1: Suppose you want to get a listing of all datasets that have SYS3 as their prefix. You can replace the LISTDS command in Figure 6.5 by one of the following:

```
LISTCAT LEVEL(SYS3)
LISTC L(SYS3)
```

The output from the LISTCAT command will be written to DDname SYSTSPRT.

Example 2: Suppose you want to rename 100 members in 'SYS3.LINKLIB'. You can have a program or a REXX exec build the control cards, which will appear as follows:

```
RENAME 'SYS3.LINKLIB(OLDNAME1)' (NEWNAME1)
RENAME 'SYS3.LINKLIB(OLDNAME2)' (NEWNAME2)
- - -
- - -
RENAME 'SYS3.LINKLIB(OLDNM100)' (NEWNM100)
```

(Note: RENAME starts in column 1 or later. These control cards will be written in an 80-byte record file. This file will then be assigned to DDname SYSTSIN in the JCL of Figure 6.5. You will then submit this job. It will perform the renaming in batch. You no longer have to manually issue 100 rename commands, one after another, on TSO or on option 3.2 of ISPF.)

Example 3: To find out the history of two members of load library 'CICS.PROD.LOADLIB', you can use the following input stream in the JCL of Figure 6.5:

```
PDS 'CICS.PROD.LOADLIB'
HIST DFHSNT
END
PDS 'CICS.PROD.LOADLIB'
HIST DFHFCTA1
END
```

(Note: As stated above, any TSO command, CLIST, or REXX exec, e.g., LISTCAT, PDS, TIME, DELETE, or RENAME, can be executed in batch. Your use of this technique can be as great and varied as your imagination allows. As shown in Example 2, you can delete or rename multiple datasets or PDS members in batch.)

Notes on running TSO commands, CLISTs, and REXX execs in TSO/E background

1. Background processing does not interfere with one's use of the terminal. Time-consuming and low-priority execs, or execs that do not require terminal interaction, can be run in the background.
2. Running an exec in the background is the same as running a CLIST or a TSO/E command. Program IKJEFT01 sets up a TSO/E environment so that you can invoke TSO commands,

```
//jobname  JOB Statement
//STEP01   EXEC PGM=IKJEFT01,DYNAMNBR=30,REGION=4096K
//SYSEXEC  DD DISP=SHR,DSN=Z1BKN.EXEC
//SYSTSPRT DD SYSOUT=*
//SYSTSIN  DD *
 EXECUTIL SEARCHDD(YES)
 %EXEC1
```

Figure 6.6.   A job that executes a REXX exec in TSO/E background.

```
//jobname  JOB Statement
//STEP01   EXEC PGM=IRXJCL,
//         PARM='TESTEXEC TEST RUN'
//SYSEXEC  DD DISP=SHR,DSN=Z1BKN.EXEC
//SYSTSPRT DD DISP=SHR,DSN=Z1BKN.SDSF.PRINT
//SYSTSIN  DD *
 data line 1
 data line 2
 data line 3
```

Figure 6.7.   A job that executes the exec of Figure 6.8 in MVS batch.

CLISTs, and REXX execs. All output is written to DDname SYSTSPRT instead of being displayed on the terminal. SYSTSPRT can be assigned to a dataset or to a SYSOUT class. For example, to use a SYSOUT class in Figure 6.5 you can comment out line 3 and uncomment line 4.

3. Figure 6.6 shows another job in which a REXX exec is executed in TSO/E background. Suppose exec EXEC1 resides in PDS 'Z1BKN.EXEC'. You can use the job shown in Figure 6.6 to execute it. You will note that the first line in the input stream is the EXECUTIL SEARCHDD command to activate SYSEXEC. This is to ensure that the system will first search DDname SYSEXEC for any exec. This command is not necessary if your system is set up to search SYSEXEC first, and then SYSPROC. The next line implicitly invokes exec EXEC1. The

system will search dataset Z1BKN.EXEC for member EXEC1 and, finding it, will execute it.

6.3.   SHOW ME THE TECHNIQUE OF EXECUTING TSO/REXX EXECS IN MVS BATCH

Let us illustrate this technique through an example. The JCL shown in Figure 6.7 executes the exec of Figure 6.8. When you submit this JCL, the output lines written to DDname SYSTSPRT will be as shown in Figure 6.9. Let us now try to understand this technique. In the JCL, we execute program IRXJCL, which is the program for executing execs in MVS batch. The parameter passed to IRXJCL in this example is 'TESTEXEC TEST RUN'. This tells

```
01     /********************* REXX **************************/
02     /* This exec receives INDATA from the argument        */
03     /* specified on the EXEC statment in the JCL. It pulls */
04     /* data items from the input stream (DDname SYSTSIN).  */
05     /* It sends a condition code which can be used in the  */
06     /* JCL on the COND operand of EXEC statement of        */
07     /* subsequent job steps.                               */
08     /*****************************************************/
09     /* Author: Barry K. Nirmal                             */
10     /*****************************************************/
11     TRACE ERROR
12     SAY 'Now Running Exec TESTEXEC'
13     ADDRESS MVS
14     PARSE ARG INDATA
15     SAY INDATA
16     parse pull datain
17     DO while DATAIN \= ''
18       say datain                    /* Pull data from SYSTSIN */
19       parse pull datain
20     END
21     SAY 'NOW LEAVING REXX EXEC TESTEXEC'
22     EXIT 110
```

Figure 6.8.   A REXX exec that is executed in MVS batch by the job shown in Figure 6.7.

```
Now Running Exec TESTEXEC
TEST RUN
 data line 1
 data line 2
 data line 3
NOW LEAVING REXX EXEC TESTEXEC
```

Figure 6.9.   Output written on SYSTSPRT when the job shown in Figure 6.7 is run.

IRXJCL to search the PDS allocated to SYSEXEC for member TESTEXEC and execute it, passing it two arguments, TEST and RUN. In this example, the system will search Z1BKN.EXEC for member TESTEXEC and execute it. This exec is shown in Figure 6.8.

When this exec starts running, on line 12 it writes the following line to DDname SYSTSPRT:

```
Now Running Exec TESTEXEC
```

This line is written starting at column 1 of the record, even if the dataset allocated to SYSTSPRT has record format of FBA. Then on line 13 the ADDRESS instruction is used to establish MVS as the host environment. On the next line the ARG instruction will place the argument specified on the PARM in the JCL in INDATA, which now will contain the value: 'TEST RUN'. On the next line the content of INDATA is written out to SYSTSPRT. On line 16 we read the first line from the input stream. In the DO loop started on line 17 we first write the content of DATAIN and then read the next record from the input stream (i.e., DDname SYSTSIN). This means that all records will be read from the input stream and written out to SYSTSPRT. Finally, on line 21 we write the following line on SYSTSPRT:

```
NOW LEAVING REXX EXEC TESTEXEC
```

On line 22 the EXIT instruction is executed with return code 110. The job step ends with condition code of 110. This means that in the job output you will find the following line:

```
jobname STEP01 - STEP WAS EXECUTED - COND CODE 0110
```

This condition code can be used to bypass or execute other job steps that might follow the step where IRXJCL is executed.

6.4. CAN THE DATA STACK BE USED WHEN RUNNING AN EXEC IN TSO/E BACKGROUND OR MVS BATCH IN THE SAME WAY AS IN TSO/E FOREGROUND?

Yes; when you run an exec in the TSO/E background, or MVS batch, the data stack is used in the same way as in TSO/E foreground. However, the PULL instruction works differently when the stack is empty. In the TSO/E foreground, PULL goes to the terminal for input. In the TSO/E background and MVS batch, PULL goes to the input stream, that is, DDname SYSTSIN. When there is no data in the input stream, the PULL returns a null. This means that when the end-of-file has been reached on the input stream, and the PULL instruction is in a loop, an infinite loop can occur. For example, the following code will result in an infinite loop when executed in TSO/E background or MVS batch, assuming that end-of- file had been reached on SYSTSIN before it was executed:

```
DO WHILE DATAIN = ''
  PULL DATAIN
END
```

But this code will work fine when run in TSO/E foreground.

6.5. COMPARE TSO/E BACKGROUND (IKJEFT01) WITH MVS BATCH (IRXJCL) FOR EXECUTING REXX EXECS

The following describes the similarities and differences between running an exec in the TSO/E background and running it in MVS batch:

1. In both cases, execs run without terminal interaction.
2. In both cases, the default DDnames are SYSTSPRT for output and SYSTSIN for input.

3. In both cases, JCL should be stored in a fixed-blocked, 80-byte record dataset.

4. In both TSO/E background and MVS batch, an exec can contain:
   - REXX instructions
   - TSO/E REXX commands, e.g., EXECIO, NEWSTACK, DELSTACK

   In TSO/E background only, an exec can also contain:
   - TSO/E commands, e.g., TIME, LISTC, LISTDS
   - TSO/E external functions, e.g., LISTDSI, MSG, SYSDSN, SYSVAR

5. In TSO/E background, execs are invoked through the PARM parameter on the EXEC statement and through explicitly or implicitly using the EXEC command in the input stream. In MVS batch, execs are invoked only through the PARM parameter on the EXEC statement. The first word on the PARM parameter is the PDS member name that is to be executed, and the subsequent words are the arguments to be passed to the exec.

6. In TSO/E background, the information in the input stream is processed mainly as TSO/E commands and invocations of execs and CLISTs. (They can also be used as input data for the exec that is running, if the exec issues a PULL instruction and the data stack is empty.) In MVS batch, the information in the input stream is processed only as input data for the exec that is being run.

7. In TSO/E background, an exec to be executed can be either a PDS member or a sequential dataset. In MVS batch, an exec to be executed must be a PDS member.

8. In both TSO/E background and MVS batch, output is sent to DDname SYSTSPRT, which can be assigned to a output dataset or a SYSOUT class.

9. In TSO/E background, messages are displayed in the output file (SYSTSPRT). In MVS batch, output may appear in the JCL output listing and in the output file (SYSTSPRT). To prevent messages from appearing in the output file, use the TRACE OFF instruction.

6.6. SHOW ME HOW TO ADD A REXX EXEC AS A COMMAND IN THE ISPF COMMAND TABLE

Suppose you have developed a REXX exec that can be invoked by entering the following on the command line of any ISPF panel:

```
TSO MEX
```

You can add this command to the ISPF command table so that you can merely enter MEX on the command line of any ISPF panel to execute it. To illustrate the technique of adding a command to the ISPF command table, let me explain how I helped John do it. John wanted to add command BKN to the ISPF command table so that it would invoke REXX exec BKNEXEC. He was accessing ISPF by issuing the following command in his startup CLIST:

```
ISPSTART PANEL(ISR@PRIM) NEWAPPL(SYS)
```

(He could also issue this command from native TSO, i.e., from the READY prompt.) Here, the NEWAPPL operand specifies SYS as the application-id. So, the system was using member SYSCMDS as the application command table name. John had the following datasets allocated to ISPTLIB, the input table library:

```
SYS1.ISPTLIB
SYS1.ISRTLIB
SYS1.ISFTLIB
```

(The first two datasets are for ISPF/PDF and the third is for SDSF.) He had no dataset allocated to ISPTABL, the output table library. In SYS1.ISPTLIB, member SYSCMDS was there containing application commands, and member ISPCMDS was there containing system commands. (The system command table, ISPCMDS, is always in use by ISPF.) When John entered BKN as a command on any ISPF panel, member SYSCMDS of SYS1.ISPTLIB was searched first, and then the system command table ISPCMDS in SYS1.ISPTLIB was searched. Not finding this command in either of these two tables, the system rejected it as an invalid command. John wanted to add BKN as a new command to SYSCMDS. We know that ISPF command tables are modified using option 3.9 (Command Table Utility) of ISPF/PDF. But when he accessed

ISPF option 3.9 and entered SYS as the application name, the system displayed the contents of SYSCMDS, but with the message that this command table was open and hence could not be modified. I had John do the following:

- Allocate Z1JHN.ISPTLIB as a PDS with logical record length of 80, where Z1JHN is John's TSO prefix.
- Change his startup CLIST so that ISPTLIB, the input table library, was now allocated to Z1JHN.ISPTLIB followed by the three libraries mentioned above. Now ISPTLIB would be allocated to the following datasets:

```
Z1JHN.ISPTLIB
SYS1.ISPTLIB
SYS1.ISRTLIB
SYS1.ISFTLIB
```

- Change his startup CLIST so that ISPTABL, the output table library, was allocated to Z1JHN.ISPTLIB, the same dataset allocated as the first dataset of ISPTLIB concatenation.
- Using ISPF 3.3, copy SYSCMDS from SYS1.ISPTLIB in member SYSNCMDS in Z1JHN.ISPTLIB.
- Modify table SYSNCMDS. To do so, he had to go to option 3.9 (Command Table Utility) of ISPF/PDF and specify SYSN as application-id. When the system displayed the command table, John went to the end of the file and inserted the following entry (see italic type):

```
VERB   T   ACTION
               DESCRIPTION
BKN    0   SELECT CMD(BKNEXEC)
               BARRY NIRMAL'S EXTENDED EDIT/BROWSE
```

- Press the END key to save the changed table.
- Change his startup CLIST, so that the last command is changed from

```
ISPSTART PANEL(ISR@PRIM) NEWAPPL(SYS)
               to
ISPSTART PANEL(ISR@PRIM) NEWAPPL(SYSN)
```

- Log off TSO and log onto TSO again.

Now ISPF is initialized with application ID being SYSN. When John enters BKN on the command line of any ISPF panel, ISPF searches the application table SYSNCMDS in datasets allocated to ISPTLIB. Finding this table in Z1JHN.ISPTLIB, the system searches it for command BKN. Finding this command there, it takes the specified action, which in this case is to invoke a REXX exec or CLIST named BKNEXEC.

Now suppose John is on native TSO, and he enters ISPF to access ISPF. In this case, ISPF will be started but the default application will be ISP. When John enters BKN as a command, the system would now search member ISPCMDS in the datasets allocated to ISPTLIB. Failing to find command BKN in the table, it would reject the command.

Hopefully, the above procedure has explained the technique of adding or updating the ISPF command table. Here is the system mechanism in summary form: When you specify xxxx as application-id on ISPF 3.9 (Command Table Utility), the system interprets it as your wish to display or modify the ISPF command table named xxxxCMDS. (xxxx can be a string of 1 to 4 characters.) It searches the libraries allocated to ISPTLIB for member xxxxCMDS and displays its content. When you modify the table and press the END key, the modified table is written to the library allocated to ISPTABL as member xxxxCMDS. Only one PDS can be allocated to ISPTABL, but one or more PDSs can be allocated to ISPTLIB, as shown above.

What is the advantage of adding a command to the ISPF command table? Consider the exec of Figures 3.20 and 3.22 in Chapter 3. It displays a panel where you can select any of the 30 datasets for edit or browse. If this exec is entered in ISPF command table as, say, EBE (Extended Browse/Edit), you can simply enter EBE on the command line of any ISPF panel to invoke it. When you press the END key on the extended edit/browse panel, you will return to the panel where you had entered EBE. This makes it easy for you to pop in and out of the extended edit/browse facility.

APPENDIX **A**

Summary of REXX
Built-In Functions

REXX provides over 50 built-in functions that fall into the following categories:

- Arithmetic functions
  These functions evaluate numbers from the argument and return a particular value.

- Comparison functions
  These functions compare numbers and/or strings and return a value.

- Conversion functions
  These functions convert one type of data representation to another type of data representation.

- Formatting functions
  These functions manipulate the characters and spacing in strings supplied in the argument.

- String manipulating functions
  These functions analyze a string supplied in the argument (or a variable representing a string) and return a particular value.

- Miscellaneous functions
  These functions do not clearly fit into any of the other categories.

The following tables briefly describe the functions in each category. For a complete description of these functions, see *TSO/E Version 2 REXX Reference*.

ARITHMETIC FUNCTIONS

Function	Description
ABS	Returns the absolute value of a number.
DIGITS	Returns the current setting of NUMERIC DIGITS.
FORM	Returns the current setting of NUMERIC FORM.
FUZZ	Returns the current setting of NUMERIC FUZZ.
MAX	Returns the largest number from the input list of numbers.
MIN	Returns the smallest number from the input list of numbers.
RANDOM	Returns a pseudo-random, non-negative whole number in the range specified.
SIGN	Returns −1, 0, or 1, which indicates the sign of the input number.
TRUNC	Returns the integer part of the input number and a particular number of decimal places, if specified.

COMPARISON FUNCTIONS

Function	Description
COMPARE	Returns 0 if the two input strings are identical. If the strings are not identical, the returned number is the column position of the first character that does not match.
DATATYPE	Checks for a particular type of input, such as number or character.
SYMBOL	Analyzes the input word and returns VAR (if it is an assigned variable name), LIT (if it is a constant symbol or an unassigned variable name), or BAD (if it is not a valid REXX symbol).

CONVERSION FUNCTIONS

Function	Description
C2D	Converts a character string to a decimal number. (Character to Decimal)
C2X	Converts a character string to its hexadecimal representation. (Character to Hexadecimal)
D2C	Converts a decimal number to a character string. (Decimal to Character)
D2X	Converts a decimal number to a string of hexadecimal characters. (Decimal to Hexadecimal)
X2C	Converts hexadecimal characters to a character string. (Hexadecimal to Character)
X2D	Converts hexadecimal characters to a decimal number. (Hexadecimal to Decimal)

FORMATTING FUNCTIONS

Function	Description
CENTER/ CENTRE	Centers the input string in the specified length with pad characters added as needed.
COPIES	Repeats the input string a specified number of times.
FORMAT	Rounds and formats the input number.
JUSTIFY	Formats blank-delimited words in the input string by adding the specified pad characters between words to extend the string to both margins.
LEFT	Returns a string of specified length, truncated or padded on the right as needed.
RIGHT	Returns a string of specified length, truncated or padded on the left as needed.
SPACE	Formats the blank-delimited words in the input string with a specified number of pad characters between each word.

STRING MANIPULATING FUNCTIONS

Function	Description
ABBREV	Checks if one string is equal to the specified number of leading characters of another string. Returns 1 if they are equal and 0 if they are not.
DELSTR	Deletes a specified number of characters from a string starting at a specified point in the string.
DELWORD	Deletes a specified number of words from a string starting at a specified word in the string.
FIND	Searches the input string for the first occurrence of a specified phrase and returns the number of the word in the string where the phrase is found.
INDEX	Searches an input string (string 1) for the first occurrence of another input string (string 2), and returns the character position in string 1 where string 2 is found.
INSERT	Inserts one input string into another string after a specified character position.
LASTPOS	Searches an input string (string 1) for the last occurrence of another input string (string 2) and returns the character position in string 1 where string 2 last occurs.
LENGTH	Returns the length of the input string.
OVERLAY	Places an input string (string 1) on top of another input string (string 2) starting at a specified character position.
POS	Returns the position of one string in another.
REVERSE	Reverses an input string.
STRIP	Removes characters from the input string based on the option specified.
SUBSTR	Returns a portion of the input string beginning at a specified character position.
SUBWORD	Returns a portion of the input string starting at a specified word number.
TRANSLATE	Translates characters in an input string to other specified characters.

Function	Description
VERIFY	Verifies that an input string (string 1) is composed only of characters from another input string (string 2). If a character in string 1 is not found in string 2, the function returns the character position of the first unmatched character.
WORD	Returns a word from an input string indicated by a specified number.
WORDINDEX	Returns the column position in an input string of a specified word.
WORDLENGTH	Returns the length of a specified word (indicated by word number) from the input string.
WORDPOS	Returns the number position of a specified word in the input string.
WORDS	Returns the number of blank-delimited words in the input string.

MISCELLANEOUS FUNCTIONS

Function	Description
ADDRESS	Returns the environment to which host commands are sent.
ARG	Returns information about the argument strings to an exec, function, or subroutine.
BITAND	Returns a string composed of two input strings logically ANDed together, bit by bit.
BITOR	Returns a string composed of two input strings logically ORed together, bit by bit.
BITXOR	Returns a string composed of two input strings exclusive ORed together, bit by bit.
DATE	Returns the date in various optional formats.
ERRORTEXT	Returns the error message associated with the specified error number.
EXTERNALS	Returns the number of items waiting to be displayed on the terminal screen. In TSO/E, this function always returns a 0.

Function	Description
LINESIZE	Returns the current terminal line width.
QUEUED	Returns the number of items remaining in the data stack.
SOURCELINE	Returns either the last line in the source file or the line specified by number.
TIME	Returns the time in either the 24-hour clock format, or one of many optional formats.
TRACE	Returns the trace actions currently in effect.
USERID	Returns the system-defined user identifier.
VALUE	Returns the value of a specified symbol.
XRANGE	Returns a string of all one-byte codes between and including a specified starting value and an ending value.

Examples of Using
REXX Built-In Functions

In this appendix, we present all the built-in functions (except for one or two) of the REXX language. TSO/E external functions are not given. Each function is described in the summary form followed usually by a short piece of code that illustrates its use. You can copy the code accompanying each function to a member of a PDS that is allocated to DDname SYSEXEC during your TSO session. You may then execute that member (e.g., TEST1) to verify that the results displayed are as given below. All the exec examples given below have been tested under TSO/E.

ABBREV(information, info, length)   length is optional.

Returns 1 if info is equal to the leading characters of information and the length of info is not less than length. Returns 0 if either of these conditions is not met.

length, if specified, must be a nonnegative whole number. The default for length is the number of characters in info. A null string will always match if a length of 0 (or the default) is used. This allows you to select a default keyword automatically if the user entered a null response. For example, ABBREV('DISPLAY',ans) = 1 if the content of ans is null. Note the following:

```
ABBREV('DISPLAY','Dis')   --------> 0
ABBREV('DISPLAY','DIS')   --------> 1
ABBREV('DISPLAY','DISPLAY1')   --> 0
```

Here is a small piece of tested code:

```
Say 'Enter DISPLAY or its abbreviation to display',
'the record: '
Say '(You can enter your answer in upper or' 'lower
case)'
Pull answer
If Abbrev('DISPLAY',answer,1) = 1 then
   say 'OK the record will be displayed'
else say 'The record will not be displayed'
```

ABS(number)

Returns the absolute value of a number. Consider these examples:

```
ABS('120.4')      ---->  120.4
ABS(' -  12.1')   ---->   12.1
```

Here is a small piece of tested code:

```
number = -110
if abs(number) < 200 then
   say 'absolute value of number is less than 200'
else say 'absolute value of number is 200 or more'
```

ADDRESS()

Returns the name of the environment to which host commands are being sent. Consider the following code:

```
A = address()
Say 'The current host environment is = ' A
/* Now change host command environment to ISPF */
address ispexec
A = address()
Say 'The current host environment is = ' A
```

If you execute this code, the result displayed will be:

```
The current host environment is  = TSO
The current host environment is  = ISPEXEC
```

ARG(*n*,option)   *n* and option are optional.

If no parameter is given, returns the number of arguments passed to the program or internal routine. If only *n* is given, the *n*th argument is returned. If the argument string does not exist, a null string is returned.

Example 1: Suppose the following code was called using "CALL name;", i.e., without specifying any arguments.

```
a = arg()
b = arg(1)
say a b
```

If this code is executed, a will be set to 0, and b will be set to a null string.

Example 2: Suppose the code shown in Example 1 is called using "Call name Harry Smith;"

When it is executed, a will contain 1 and b will contain 'HARRY SMITH'.

Example 3: Suppose the code shown in Example 1 is called using "Call name 'Harry Smith' ;"

When it is executed, a will contain 1 and b will contain 'Harry Smith'.

Example 4: Suppose the code shown in Example 1 is called using "Call name Harry, Smith;"

When it is executed, a will contain 2 and b will contain 'HARRY'.

BITAND(string1,string2,pad) string2 and pad are optional.

Returns a string composed of the two strings logically ANDed together bit by bit. The length of the output string is the length of the longer of the two. If pad is given, the shorter string is extended to right using the pad character, before applying the logical operation. If no pad character is given the AND operation terminates when the shorter of the two strings is exhausted, and the unprocessed portion of the longer string is appended to the partial result. If string is not specified, it defaults to a null string (of length zero). Consider the following exec:

```
a = '73'x
b = '27'x
c =  bitand(a,b)
d = c2x(c)
say d
```

If this code is executed, it will display '23', showing that the content of c is '23'x.

BITOR(string1,string2,pad) string2 and pad are optional.

Returns a string composed of the two strings logically ORed together bit by bit. The length of the output string is the length of the longer of the two. If pad is given, the shorter string is extended to right using the pad character, before applying the logical operation. If no pad character is given, the OR operation terminates when the shorter of the two strings is exhausted, and the unprocessed portion of the longer string is appended to the partial result. If string is not specified, it defaults to a null string (of length zero). Consider the following exec:

```
a = '15'x
b = '24'x
c =  bitor(a,b)
d = c2x(c)
say d
```

If this code is executed, it will display '35', showing that the content of c is '35'x.

BITXOR(string1,string2,pad)   string2 and pad are optional.

Returns a string composed of the two strings logically exclusive ORed together bit by bit. The length of the output string is the length of the longer of the two. If pad is given, the shorter string is extended to right using the pad character, before applying the logical operation. If no pad character is given, the exclusive OR operation terminates when the shorter of the two strings is exhausted, and the unprocessed portion of the longer string is appended to the partial result. If string is not specified, it defaults to a null string (of length zero).

```
a = '12'x
b = '22'x
c =  bitxor(a,b)
d = c2x(c)
say d
```

If this code is executed, it will display '30', showing that the content of c is '30'x.

CENTER/CENTRE(string,length,pad)   pad is optional.

Returns a string of length length with string centered in it, with pad characters added as necessary to make up length. The default pad character is blank. Consider the following exec:

```
A = 'Barry Nirmal'
B = center(a,20,'-')
say B
```

If you execute it, the result displayed will be:

```
----Barry Nirmal----
```

COMPARE(string1,string2,pad)   pad is optional.

Compares the two strings, padding the shorter string on the right with pad if necessary. If the two strings are equal, returns 0, otherwise returns the position of the first character that does not match.

```
a = 'Barry'
b = 'BARRY'
c = 'BARRY '
x = compare(a,b)
y = compare(b,c)
z = compare('ab-- ','ab','-')
say x
say y
say z
```

When you execute this code, it will display 2 for x, 0 for y, and 5 for z.

COPIES(string,n)

Returns n concatenated copies of string. n must be a nonnegative whole number.

```
a = 'Barry '
b = copies(a,3)
say b
```

If you execute this code, the result displayed will be:

```
Barry Barry Barry
```

C2D(string,n)   n is optional.

Converts string into decimal. For example, consider the following exec:

```
A = 'a'
b = '81'x
x = c2d(a)
y = c2d(b)
Say 'a = ' a
say 'x = ' x
Say 'b = ' b
say 'y = ' y
```

When it is executed, the output will appear as follows:

```
a = a
x = 129
b = a
y = 129
```

C2X(string)

Converts a character string into its hexadecimal representation.
For example, consider this code:

```
A = '72s'
b = c2x(a)
Say 'a = ' a
Say 'b = ' b
```

When it is executed, the output will appear as follows:

```
a = 72s
b = F7F2A2
```

DATATYPE(string,type)   type is optional.

If only string is specified, the returned result is NUM if string is
a valid REXX number; otherwise the returned result is CHAR.

If type is specified, the returned result is 1 if string matches
the type; otherwise a 0 is returned. If string is null, 0 is returned,
except when type is X, when 1 is returned. Type must be specified

in uppercase only, and it is A for alphanumeric, B for bits, L for lowercase, M for mixedcase, N for number, U for uppercase, W for whole number X for hexadecimal, etc.

Example 1

```
a = 'Barry'
say 'a is of datatype: ' datatype(a)
```

This code will display CHAR as datatype of a.

Example 2

```
a = '100'
say 'a is of datatype: ' datatype(a)
```

This code will display NUM as datatype of a.

Example 3

```
a = '1.1'
If datatype(a) = 'NUM' Then Say 'a is numeric'
If datatype(a) = 'num' Then Say 'a is numeric'
```

Here the first test will be true but the second will be false.

Example 4

```
a = '1,1'
b = datatype(a,'N')    /* check if a is numeric */
say 'b = ' b
c = datatype(a,'A')    /* check if a is alphanumeric */
say 'c = ' c
```

This code will display 0 as the value of b and c.

DATE(option)   option is optional.

Returns the system date in the format 'dd mon yyyy', e.g., 12 Dec 1991. Consider the following exec:

```
a = date()
say A
a = date('J')   /* Julian */
say A
a = date('U')   /* USA */
say a
a = date('E')   /* European Format */
say a
```

If you execute this code, the result displayed will be as follows:

```
31 Dec 1991
91365
12/31/91
31/12/19
```

DELSTR(string,*n*,length)   length is optional.

Deletes the substring of string that begins at the *n*th character, and is of length length. If length is not specified, the rest of the string is deleted. If *n* is greater than the length of string, the string is returned unchanged. Consider the following exec:

```
A = 'Barry K. Nirmal'
B = delstr(a,6)
Say B
```

This code when executed will display the following:

```
Barry
```

DELWORD(string,*n*,length)   length is optional.

Deletes the substring of string that begins at the *n*th word. The length refers to the number of blank-delimited words that are to be deleted. length can be more than the number of words available for deletion. If length is omitted, the remaining words in string are deleted. If *n* is greater than the number of words in string, string is returned unchanged. Consider the following exec:

```
A = 'Barry K. Nirmal'
B = delword(a,2)
Say B
A = 'Barry K. Nirmal'
B = delword(a,2,9)
Say B
A = 'Barry K. Nirmal'
B = delword(a,4)
Say B
```

This code when executed will display the following:

```
Barry
Barry
Barry K. Nirmal
```

DIGITS()

Returns the current setting of NUMERIC DIGITS. Consider the following exec:

```
Say 'The current setting is ' digits()
Numeric digits 11
Say 'The current setting is ' digits()
```

This code when run will display the following:

```
The current setting is 9
The current setting is 11
```

D2C(wholenumber,*n*)   *n* is optional.

Decimal-to-character conversion. If *n* is specified, it is the length of the final result in characters. Consider the following exec:

```
a = 129
b = d2c(a)
c = d2c(a,2)
```

When this exec is run, b will be set to '81'x. Its length will be 1. And c will be set to '0081'x. Its length will be 2.

D2X(wholenumber,*n*)   *n* is optional.

Decimal-to-hexadecimal conversion. If *n* is specified, it is the length of the final result in characters. If *n* is not specified, the result is such that there are no leading 0 characters. Consider this exec:

```
a = 120
b = d2x(a)
say 'Decimal ' a ' = Hexadecimal ' b
```

If this exec is executed, it will display the following:

```
Decimal 120 = Hexadecimal 78
```

FIND(string,phrase)

Instead of FIND, use function WORDPOS for this kind of word search. WORDPOS is described later.

FORM()

Returns the current setting of NUMERIC FORM.

```
say 'The current setting is ' form()
Numeric form Engineering
Say 'The current setting is ' form()
```

This code when run will display the following:

```
The current setting is SCIENTIFIC
The current setting is ENGINEERING
```

FUZZ()

Returns the current setting of NUMERIC FUZZ.

```
Say 'The current setting is ' fuzz()
Numeric fuzz 2
Say 'The current setting is ' fuzz()
```

This code when run will display the following:

```
The current setting is 0
The current setting is 2
```

INDEX(haystack,needle,start)   start is optional.

Returns the position of one string, needle, into another string, haystack. If the string needle is not found, 0 is returned. If start is not given, search starts at the first character of haystack. If start is given, search starts at the position specified by it. Consider the following exec:

```
a1 = 'barry'
a2 = 'Barry
a3 = 'Nirmal'
name = 'Barry K. Nirmal'
b = index(name,a1)
c = index(name,a2)
d = index(name,a3)
say b c d
```

If this code is executed, it will display '0 1 10'. You may use POS instead of INDEX for obtaining the position of one string in another.

INSERT(new,target,*n*, length,pad)   *n*,   length, and pad are optional.

---

n is the number of characters to leave from the beginning of string target before inserting the string new into the string target, padded to length length. The default pad character is a blank. The default value for *n* is zero. If *n* is greater than the length of the target string, padding is added there also.

Example

```
first = 'B'
middle =' K'
last = ' Nirmal'
name = ''
name = insert(last,name)
name = insert(middle,name,,3,'.')
name = insert(first,name,,2,'.')
say name
```

When this code is executed, it will display 'B. K. Nirmal' as the value of name.

JUSTIFY(string,length,pad)   pad is optional.

The string is first normalized as if SPACE(string) was executed. This converts multiple blanks to single blank, and removes leading and trailing blanks. If length is less than the width of the normalized string, the string is then truncated on the right and any trailing blank is removed. Then the system adds extra pad characters evenly from left to right to provide the required length, and the blanks between words are replaced with the pad character. Consider the following exec:

```
a = 'ABC CO'
b = justify(a,10)
c = justify(a,5,'$')
say b
say c
```

If this code is executed, it will display:

```
ABC     CO
ABC$C
```

LASTPOS(needle,haystack,start)   start is optional.

Returns the position of the last occurrence of one string, needle, into another string, haystack. If string needle is not found, it returns 0. If start is not given, search starts in the backward direction starting at the last character of haystack. If start is given, search starts in the backward direction starting at the specified position. start defaults to the length of the string if it is larger than this value.

```
a1 = 'Barry'
a2 = 'Nirmal'
a3 = ' '
name = 'Barry K. Nirmal'
b =   lastpos(a1,name)
c =   lastpos(a2,name)
d =   lastpos(a3,name)
say b c d
```

If this code is executed, it will display '1 10 9'.

LEFT(string,length,pad)   pad is optional.

Returns a string of length length that contains the leftmost length characters of string. The returned string is padded with pad character, or truncated, on the right as needed. The default for pad is blank. Consider the following exec:

```
a = 'Barry K. Nirmal'
b = left(a,5)
say b
```

If you execute this code, it will display 'Barry'.

LENGTH(string)

Returns the length of string. For example, if you execute the following code:

```
a = 'Barry'
b = length(a)
say b
```

it will display 5 because the length of the string contained in a is 5.

LINESIZE()

Returns the current terminal line width minus 1. This is the point at which the system will break lines displayed using the SAY instruction. Consider this:

```
a = linesize()
say a
```

This code when executed under TSO/E will display 79 for most of the IBM 3270-type terminals.

MAX(number1,number2,.....)   number2, number3, etc. are optional.

Returns the largest number from the list specified, formatted according to the current setting of NUMERIC DIGITS. Up to 20 numbers can be specified, but by nesting calls to MAX, you can overcome this limitation. Consider the following exec:

```
a = 3
b = -3
c = 10
d = 99
res = max(a,b,c,d)
say res
```

This code when run will display 99 on your terminal.

MIN(number1,number2,.....)   number2, number3, etc. are optional.

Returns the smallest number from the list specified, formatted according to the current setting of NUMERIC DIGITS. Up to 20 numbers can be specified, but by nesting calls to MIN, you can overcome this limitation.

```
a = 3
b = -3
c = 10
d = 99
res = min(a,b,c,d)
say res
```

This code when run will display –3 on your terminal.

OVERLAY(source,target,_n_,length,pad)   _n_, length, and pad are optional.

Overlays the string target, starting at the _n_th character with the string source, padded or truncated to length length. The default for _n_ is 1 and the default pad character is a blank. If _n_ is greater than the length of string target, padding is added before string source.

```
a = 'Barry x. Nirmal'
a = Overlay('K',a,7)
say a
x = '123'
y = 'abc'
z = overlay(x,y,5,6,'$')
say z
```

If you execute this code, it will display the following:

```
Barry K. Nirmal
abc$123$$$
```

POS(needle,haystack,start)   start is optional.

Returns the position of one string, needle, into another string, haystack. If needle is not found, 0 is returned. Unless start is specified, search starts at the first character of haystack. start specifies the point at which the search is to start.

```
a = 'Nirmal'
name = 'Barry K. Nirmal'
c = pos(a,name)
say c
```

If this code is executed, it will display 10.

QUEUED()

Returns the number of lines that are in the queue when this function is executed. Note: TSO/E implementation of the queue is a data stack.

```
a = queued()
say a
push a
a = queued()
say a
Pull a
```

If you execute this code, it will display 0 on the first line and 1 on the next.

RANDOM(min,max,seed)   all the arguments are optional.

Gives you a pseudo-random number in the range min to max, inclusive. The default values for min and max are 0 and 999, respectively. Max minus min must not exceed 100000. For example, to get a random number between 10 and 20, use Random(10,20). To obtain a predictable sequence of pseudo-random numbers, use RANDOM a number of times, but specify a seed the first time only. (The seed can be anything). For example, the following code will always give you the same three numbers. But if you remove the seed from the first RANDOM, the numbers obtained will be different every time you execute this code.

```
a= random(,,1989)
say a
a= random()
say a
a = random()
say a
```

REVERSE(string)

Returns string, in reverse order.

```
a = 'Nirmal'
b = reverse(a)
say b
```

If this code is executed, it will display 'lamriN'.

RIGHT(string,length,pad)   pad is optional and defaults to blank.

Returns a string of length length that contains the rightmost length characters of string. The returned string is padded with pad character, or truncated, on the left as needed.

```
a = 'Barry K. Nirmal'
b = right(a,6)
say b
```

If you execute this code, it will display 'Nirmal'.

SIGN(number)

Returns a number that indicates the sign of number. If number is less than 0, −1 is returned; if it is 0, a 0 is returned; and if it is greater than 0, 1 is returned. Consider the following complete code:

```
a = 100
b = -109
c = sign(a)
d = sign(b)
say c d
```

When this code is executed, it will display '1 −1'.

SOURCELINE(n)   n is optional.

If you omit n, it will return the line number of the last line in the file. If you provide n, it will return you the nth line in the file.

```
a = sourceline()
b = sourceline(2)
say a
say b
```

If you copy this code in member TEST1 of a PDS that is allocated to DDname SYSEXEC, and execute it by entering TSO TEST1, you will receive the following output:

```
4
b = sourceline(2)
```

SPACE(string,n,pad)   n and pad are optional.

Formats the blank-delimited words in string with n pad characters between each word. If n is 0, all blanks are removed. Leading and trailing blanks are always removed. The default for n is 1 and the default pad character is a blank. Consider the following complete code:

```
a = 'Barry      K.      Nirmal'
b = space(a)
say b
```

If you execute this code, the result displayed will be:

```
Barry K. Nirmal
```

STRIP(string,option,char)   option and char are optional.

Removes leading and/or trailing characters from string, depending on option specified. Valid options are B for both, L for leading, and T for trailing. (The default is both.) The third argument, char, specifies the character to be removed. If omitted, char defaults to blank. If char is given, it must be exactly one character long.

```
name = '  Barry K. Nirmal  '
name = strip(name)
say name
```

If you execute this code, it will display 'Barry K. Nirmal'.

SUBSTR(string,*n*,length,pad)   length and pad are optional.

Returns that portion of string that begins at the nth character, and is of length length, padded with pad if needed. If length is omitted, the rest of the string is returned. The default pad character is a blank.

```
NAME = 'BARRY K. NIRMAL'
A = SUBSTR(NAME,7,2)
say a
```

If you execute this code, it will display 'K.'.

SUBWORD(string,*n*,length)   length is optional.

Returns one or more blank-delimited words from string that starts at the *n*th word, and is of length length, blank-delimited words. If length is omitted, it defaults to the remaining words in string. The returned word will not have leading or trailing blanks, but will include all blanks between the words chosen.

```
name = 'Barry K. Nirmal'
a= subword(name,2,1)
say a
```

If this code is executed, it will return 'K.'.

SYMBOL(name)

Returns the state of symbol named by name. If it is not a valid REXX symbol, BAD is returned. If it is the name of a variable, i.e., a symbol that has been assigned a value, VAR is returned, or else LIT is returned. LIT indicates that it is either a constant symbol or a symbol that has not yet been assigned a value, i.e., a literal.

Normally name should be specified in quotes or derived from an expression so that it does not get substituted by its value before being passed to the function. Consider the following complete code:

```
A = 3
B = symbol(a)
C = symbol('a')
D = symbol('x')
say b c d
```

If you execute this code, it will display 'LIT VAR LIT'.

TIME(option) option is optional.

If no option is specified, returns time in format hh:mm:ss (hours, minutes, and seconds), e.g., 04:12:12.

TRACE(option) option is optional.

Returns trace actions that are currently in effect.

```
a = Trace()
say a
```

If you execute this code, it will display N because trace is off.

TRANSLATE(string, tableo,tablei,pad) tableo, tablei, and pad are optional.

Translates characters in string to other characters. If neither translate table is given, string is merely converted to upper case, i.e., a lowercase a–z to uppercase A–Z.

```
name = 'Barry K. nirmal'
b = translate(name)
say b
```

If this code is executed, it will display 'BARRY K. NIRMAL'.

TRUNC(number,*n*) *n* is optional.

Returns the integer part of the number, and *n* decimal places. The default for *n* is zero, meaning that no decimal places will be returned. The number is first rounded according to the current setting of NUMERIC DIGITS, and then it is truncated to *n* decimal places. For example, consider this code:

```
a =TRUNC(120.3)
say a
a =TRUNC(123.098,2)
say a
a =TRUNC(123,2)
say a
```

If this code is executed, it will display this:

```
120
123.09
123.00
```

USERID()

Returns the TSO user ID, if the REXX exec is running under TSO. For example, the following code will display your TSO ID, if you run it, from your TSO terminal:

```
a = userid()
say a
```

VALUE(name)

Returns the value of a symbol. name must be a valid REXX symbol, or an error occurs. Like symbols appearing normally in REXX expressions, lowercase characters will be translated to upper case and substitution will occur in compound name, if possible.
Note: barry = VALUE('a') is always the same as barry = a. Hence it is not useful to entirely specify name as a quoted string.

Example 1

```
a1 = 'a'
a2 = 'b'
N = 1
X = value('A'N)
say ' X = ' X
```

When this code is executed, X will display as 'a', because the value of A1 was 'a' when the VALUE function was invoked.

As shown by this example, this function is useful when you have a number of variables, A1, A2, A3, . . . , A50, and you want to obtain the value of A*n* where *n* is any number in the range 1–50.

Example 2

```
Drop xxx
Z = value(xxx)
say ' Z = ' Z
```

When this code is executed, Z will display as 'XXX' because variable XXX was uninitialized when the VALUE function was invoked.

VERIFY(string,reference,option,start)   option and start are optional.

Verifies that string contains only characters from reference. If all the characters were found in reference, returns 0, otherwise returns the position of the first character in string that is not also in reference. The default for start is 1, meaning that the search starts at the first character of string.

```
A = 'Nirmal,B'
Ref = 'ABCDEFGHIJKLMNOPQRSTUVWXYZ'
b = Verify(a,ref)
say b
```

If you execute this code, it will display '2', because the second character of a (lowercase i) is not present in Ref.

WORD(string,*n*)

Returns the *n*th blank-delimited word in string. If string contains less than *n* words, a null string is returned. Thus, this function is exactly the same as SUBWORD(string,*n*,1).

```
name = 'Barry K. Nirmal'
a = word(name,1)
say a
```

If this code is executed, it will display 'Barry'.

WORDINDEX(string,*n*)

Returns the position of the first character in the *n*th blank-delimited word in string. If string contains less than *n* words, 0 is returned.

```
name = 'Barry K. Nirmal'
a = wordindex(name,3)
say a
```

If this code is executed, it will display 10.

WORDLENGTH(string,*n*)

Returns the length of the *n*th blank-delimited word in string. If string contains less than *n* words, 0 is returned.

```
name = 'Barry K. Nirmal'
a = wordlength(name,1)
say a
```

If this code is executed, it will display 5.

WORDPOS(phrase,string,start)   start is optional.

String is searched for the first occurrence of the sequence of blank-delimited words phrase, and returns the word number of the first word of phrase in string. Multiple blanks between words in either phrase or string are treated as a single blank for comparison purposes, but otherwise the words must match exactly. Returns 0 if phrase is not found.

If start is not specified, the search starts at the first word, or else start specifies the word at which search is to start.

```
a = 'Barry Kumar Nirmal'
b = wordpos('Barry',a)
c = wordpos('Berry',a)
d = wordpos('Barry  Kumar',a)
Say b c d
```

If this code is executed, it will display '1 0 1'.

WORDS(string)

Returns the number of blank-delimited words in string.

```
a = 'Barry K. Nirmal'
b = words(a)
Say b
```

If this code is executed, it will display 3.

XRANGE(start,end)   start and end are optional.

Returns a string of all one-byte codes between the start and end values. The default value for start is '00'x and that for end is 'FF'x. If specified, start and end must be single characters:

```
a = xrange('a','g')
say a
b = xrange('F0'x,'F5'x)
say b
```

If you execute this code, the value displayed will be:

```
abcdefg
012345
```

X2C(hexstring)

Converts hexstring, which is a string of hexadecimal characters, into character format. For example, consider the following code:

```
A = 'f7f7a2'
b = x2c(a)
Say 'a = ' a
say 'b = ' b
```

When it is executed, the output will appear as follows:

```
a = f7f7a2
b = 72s
```

X2D(hexstring)

Converts hexstring, which is a string of hexadecimal characters, into decimal format. For example, consider the following code:

```
a = '81'
b = x2d(a)
Say 'a = ' a
say 'b = ' b
```

When it is executed, the output will appear as follows:

```
a = 81
b = 129
```

Information Provided by the SYSVAR Function

The SYSVAR function together with a particular argument value can provide information about many aspects of the system. To retrieve the information, use the SYSVAR function immediately followed by an argument value enclosed in parentheses. For example, to find out the name of the logon procedure of your current session, use the SYSVAR function with the argument SYSPROC.

```
proc = SYSVAR(sysproc)
```

There are many argument values associated with the SYSVAR function. These arguments retrieve the same information about the user, the terminal, the exec, and the system as do CLIST control variables. The following tables divide the argument values into categories pertaining to the user, terminal, exec, and system.

USER INFORMATION

Argument Value	Description
SYSPREF	Prefix as defined in the user profile
SYSPROC	Logon procedure of the current session
SYSUID	User ID of the current session

TERMINAL INFORMATION

Argument Value	Description
SYSLTERM	Number of lines available on the screen
SYSWTERM	Width of the screen

EXEC INFORMATION

Argument Value	Description
SYSENV	Whether the exec is running in the foreground or the background
SYSICMD	Name by which the exec was implicitly invoked
SYSISPF	Whether ISPF is available for the exec
SYSNEST	Whether the exec was invoked from another exec or CLIST. The invocation could be implicit or explicit.
SYSPCMD	Name of the most recently executed command
SYSSCMD	Name of the most recently executed subcommand

SYSTEM INFORMATION

Argument Value	Description
SYSCPU	Number of CPU seconds during the session in the form: *seconds.hundredths of seconds*
SYSHSM	Level of Data Facility Hierarchical Storage Manager (DFHSM) installed
SYSLRACF	Level of RACF installed
SYSRACF	Whether RACF is available
SYSSRV	Number of system resource manager (SRM) service units used during the session
SYSTSOE	Level of TSO/E installed in the form: *version release modification number*

Using the LISTDSI Function

Figure D.1 describes the contents of the variables set by LISTDSI. For VSAM datasets, only the variables SYSVOLUME, SYSUNIT, and SYSDSORG are accurate; other variables are set to question marks.

Variable	Contents
SYSDSNAME	Data set name
SYSVOLUME	Volume serial ID
SYSUNIT	Device unit on which volume resides
SYSDSORG	Data set organization:
	PS – Physical sequential
	PSU – Physical sequential unmovable
	DA – Direct organization
	DAU – Direct organization unmovable
	IS – Indexed sequential
	ISU – Indexed sequential unmovable
	PO – Partitioned organization
	POU – Partitioned organization unmovable
	VS – VSAM
	??? – Unknown

Figure D.1.   Variables set by LISTDSI.   *continues*

SYSRECFM	Record format; three-character combination of the following:

	U	– Records of undefined length
	F	– Records of fixed length
	V	– Records of variable length
	T	– Records written with the track overflow feature of the device (3375 and 3380 do not support track overflow)
	B	– Records blocked
	S	– Records written as standard or spanned variable-length blocks
	A	– Records contain ASCII printer control characters
	M	– Records contain machine code control characters
	?	– Unknown

SYSLRECL	Logical record length
SYSBLKSIZE	Block size
SYSKEYLEN	Key length
SYSALLOC	Allocation, in space units
SYSUSED	Allocation used, in space units
SYSPRIMARY	Primary allocation in space units
SYSSECONDS	Secondary allocation in space units
SYSUNITS	Space units:

	CYLINDER	– Space units in cylinders
	TRACK	– Space units in tracks
	BLOCK	– Space units in blocks
	????????	– Space units are unknown

SYSEXTENTS	Number of extents used
SYSCREATE	Creation date Year/day format, for example: 1985/102
SYSREFDATE	Last referenced date Year/day format, for example: 1985/107 (Specifying DIRECTORY causes the date to be updated)
SYSEXDATE	Expiration date Year/day format, for example: 19485/365

Figure D.1.   *continues*

SYSPASSWORD Password indication:

NONE	– No password protection
READ	– Password required to read
WRITE	– Password required to write

SYSRACFA   RACF indication:

NONE	– No RACF protection
GENERIC	– Generic profile covers this data set
DISCRETE	– Discrete profile covers this data set

SYSUPDATED Change indicator:

YES	– Data set has been updated
NO	– Data set has not been updated

SYSTRKSCYL Tracks per cylinder for the unit identified in the SYSUNIT variable

SYSBLKSTRK Blocks per track for the unit identified in the SYSUNIT variable

SYSADIRBLK Directory blocks allocated—returned only for partitioned data sets when DIRECTORY is specified

SYSUDIRBLK Directory blocks used—returned only for partitioned data sets when DIRECTORY is specified

SYSMEMBERS Number of members—returned only for partitioned data sets when DIRECTORY is specified

SYSREASON LISTDSI reason code

SYSMSGLVL1 First level message if an error occurred

SYSMSGLVL2 Second level message if an error occurred

Figure D.1.   (Continued)

MESSAGES

All LISTDSI messages are set in the variables SYSMSGLVL1 and SYSMSGLVL2. See *TSO/E Version 2 Messages* for explanations of the messages.

FUNCTION CODES

Function codes from LISTDSI replace the function call. Error routines do not receive control when an exec receives a nonzero function code from LISTDSI.

LISTDSI Function Codes	
Function Code	**Meaning**
0	Normal completion
4	Some data set information is unavailable. All data set information other than directory information can be considered valid.
16	Severe error occurred. None of the variables can be considered valid.

REASON CODES

Reason codes from the LISTDSI function appear in variable SYSREASON.

LISTDSI Reason Codes	
Reason Code	**Meaning**
0	Normal completion.
1	Error parsing the function.
2	Dynamic allocation processing error (SVC 99 error).
3	The data set is a type that cannot be processed.
4	Error determining UNIT name (IEFEB4UV error).
5	Data set not cataloged (LOCATE macro error).
6	Error obtaining the data set name (OBTAIN macro error).
7	Error finding device type (DEVTYPE macro error).
8	The data set does not reside on a direct access device.
9	DFHSM migrated the data set, NORECALL prevents retrieval.
11	Directory information was requested, but you lack authority to access the data set.
12	VSAM data sets are not supported.
13	The data set could not be opened.

Reason Code	Meaning
14	Device type not found in unit control block (UCB) tables.
17	System or user abend occurred.
18	Partial data set information was obtained.
19	Data set resides on multiple volumes.
20	Device type not found in eligible device table (EDT).
21	Catalog error trying to locate the data set.
22	Volume not mounted (OBTAIN macro error).
23	Permanent I/O error on volume (OBTAIN macro error).
24	Data set not found by OBTAIN macro.
25	Data set migrated to non-DASD device.
26	Data set resides on a mass storage device.
27	No volume serial is allocated to the data set.
28	The ddname must be one to eight characters.
29	Data set name or ddname must be specified.

Index